THIS

MODERN-DAY WITCH
2024 WHEEL OF THE YEAR
PLANNER

BELONGS TO

_____

_____

_____

_____

The Modern-Day Witch

2024
WHEEL OF THE YEAR
17-MONTH PLANNER

SHAWN ROBBINS &

LEANNA GREENAWAY

STERLING ETHOS
New York

STERLING ETHOS
New York

STERLING ETHOS and the distinctive Sterling Ethos logo
are registered trademarks of Sterling Publishing Co., Inc.

Portions of this text were published by Sterling Ethos, in *Wiccapedia*, text
© 2011 Shawn Robbins and Leanna Greenaway; *The Witch's Way*, text © 2019 by Shawn Robbins
and Leanna Greenaway; *The Crystal Witch*, text © 2019 Shawn Robbins and Leanna Greenaway;
and *The Holistic Witch*, text © 2022 Shawn Robbins and Leanna Greenaway

This publication includes alternative therapies that have not been scientifically tested, is intended
for informational purposes only, and is not intended to provide or replace conventional medical
advice, treatment or diagnosis or be a substitute to consulting with licensed medical or health-care
providers. The publisher does not claim or guarantee any benefits, healing, cure or any results in
any respect and shall not be liable or responsible for any use or application of any content in this
publication in any respect including without limitation any adverse effects, consequence, loss or
damage of any type resulting or arising from, directly or indirectly, any use or application of any
content herein. Any trademarks are the property of their respective owners, are used for editorial
purposes only, and the publisher makes no claim of ownership and shall acquire no right, title or
interest in such trademarks by virtue of this publication.

ISBN 978-1-4549-4909-1

Printed in Malaysia

2 4 6 8 10 9 7 5 3 1
unionsquareandco.com

Cover design by Elizabeth Lindy
Interior design by Jordan Wannemacher,
Elizabeth Lindy, and Jo Obarowski; layout by Westchester Publishing Services

Contents

Introduction

There is no better way to mark special dates in the calendar than with a variety of annual festivities. Over the years and with each religion, celebrations evolved to suit specific faiths and cultures. (Many Christian holidays are derived from an ancient pagan faith ritual, for instance—Easter, discussed on pages 6–7, is a perfect example.) Wiccans and witches, however, are more inclined to follow traditional customs as originally celebrated, a cycle celebrated through festivals and Sabbats that occur during what we call the Wheel of the Year. While the following pages encapsulate a general overview of significant Wiccan dates, the history and traditions, deities worshiped, and rituals performed can vary from culture to culture.

THE WHEEL OF THE YEAR

The solstice and equinox descriptions in this book correspond to the Northern Hemisphere; in the Southern Hemisphere, the solstices and equinoxes are opposite; for example, Yule in the Southern Hemisphere is the longest day of the year. As noted on page 6, the Wheel of the Year typically begins at Yule, the winter solstice, which can range from December 20–23, depending on the year. This planner begins in August 2023 and runs through December 2024, providing five additional months for planning and tracking both important festivals and everyday tasks and rituals. Each month starts off with a full monthly view calendar to give you an overview of key days for that month. (Note: Moon phases are set in Eastern Standard and adjusted for Daylight Saving Time.)

Yule
Dec 20–23
Winter Solstice

Imbolc
Feb 2
Spring Begins

Samhain
Oct 31
New Year

Ostara
Mar 19–23
Spring Equinox

Mabon
Sep 20–23
Autumn Equinox

Beltane
Apr 30–May 1
May Day

Lughnasadh
July 31–Aug 1
First Harvest

Litha
June 19–25
Summer Solstice

YULE (Winter Solstice) • December 20–23

Yule initially began with the earliest winter solstice festivals, in pre-Christian Northern Europe. It celebrated the shortest and darkest time of the year, during which the death of the old god and the birth of the new Sun King was commemorated. It is common practice to place shining objects on the altar, such as glitter, yellow candles, or sparkly, adorned ornaments. These signify the return of sun.

YULETIDE ELEMENTS AND TRADITIONS

BELLS ✦ CANDLES: Blue, green, red ✦ CRYSTALS: Black onyx, citrine, clear quartz, garnet, green tourmaline, pearl, peridot, ruby, diamond ✦ DEITIES: Green Man, Holly King, Oak King, Triple Goddess (Pagan/Celtic) Demeter, (Greek); Isis, Ra (Egyptian); Odin (Germanic/Norse) ✦ HERBS: Bay, cinnamon, evergreen, frankincense, sage ✦ Incense: Bayberry, cedar, cinnamon, pine ✦ PLANTS: poinsettia, holly, Christmas cactus, ivy ✦ Wreaths

IMBOLC • February 2

The Old Irish word *imbolc* translates to "in the belly of the mother," meaning that with the onset of spring, new life is expected. Imbolc, which corresponds with the Christian holiday Candlemas—midway between the winter solstice and spring equinox—marks a crucial time within the Wheel of the Year for fertility and growth. This tradition honors Brigid, the Celtic triple pagan goddess of healing and the hearth, who shares her name with Saint Brigid of Kildare, so it is also known as St. Brigid's Day.

IMBOLC ELEMENTS AND TRADITIONS

CANDLES: Pink, white, yellow ✦ CRYSTALS: Moonstone, rose quartz, jade ✦ DEITIES: Brigid (Pagan/Celtic) ✦ FLOWERS: Daffodil, iris, peony, violet ✦ HERBS: Angelica, basil, bay ✦ INCENSE: Cinnamon, myrrh, vanilla ✦ SPRING POPPET (white, pink, red, or yellow cloth doll filled with herbs) ✦ SWAN FEATHERS (to represent devotion) ✦ TREES: Rowan, weeping willow

OSTARA (Spring Equinox) • March 19–23

The warmth begins to wax and light overshadows the darkness—the spring equinox is approaching. Although Easter was adopted as a Christian festival, the word "Easter" derives from the Germanic goddess Éostre, goddess of the dawn, spring, and fertility. The pagan Sabbat of Ostara (also called Eostre or Eastre) was a fertile time, symbolizing the birth of all things new.

OSTARA ELEMENTS AND TRADITIONS
CANDLES: Pale green, purple, yellow ◆ CRYSTALS: Amazonite, azurite, citrine, lapis lazuli ◆ DEITIES: Freya (Norse), Ostara (Germanic), Osiris (Egyptian) ◆ EGGS (symbol of new life) ◆ HARE (a lunar animal sacred to Ostara) ◆ HERBS: Lavender, lilac, tarragon, thyme ◆ FLOWERS: Daffodil, crocus, violet, and pussy willow ◆ OSTARA BUNS (hot cross buns) ◆ TREES: Ash, alder, birch

BELTANE (May Day) • April 30–May 1
Beltane, a Gaelic fire festival, translates as "bright fire." It is usually celebrated halfway between the spring equinox and the summer solstice, and coincides with May Day. Beltane is a favorite Sabbat among witches. It marks the beginning of summer and is a time to rejoice in warmer weather, a fruitful growing season, and, hopefully, happy times to come. Sexuality, love, and fertility are also emphasized.

BELTANE ELEMENTS AND TRADITIONS
BASKETS (wicker, with flowers inside) ◆ BONFIRES ◆ CANDLES: Green, red, silver, white ◆ CROWNS (crafted from wire, decorated with flowers) ◆ CRYSTALS: Carnelian, malachite, tiger's eye ◆ DEITIES: Belenus, Green Man (Pagan/Celtic); Flora (Roman) ◆ FAERIES ◆ FLOWERS: Bluebell, rose, marigold, pansy ◆ HERBS: Lilac, mugwort, rosemary ◆ INCENSE: Jasmine, musk, rose ◆ MAYPOLES ◆ RAINWATER (for anointing candles) ◆ RIBBONS: Blue, green, purple, red, yellow, white ◆ TREES: Ash, hawthorn, oak

LITHA (Summer Solstice) • June 19–25
Litha marks the summer solstice, or Midsummer—which brings us the longest days and shortest nights (though the dates do vary with geography and culture). Everything in the world is blooming with fruitfulness, the goddess is heavily pregnant with child, and the sun god is at his peak of virility. From here on, as the sun begins to wane, the days will become shorter and the nights longer, and soon the cycle of life will be complete.

LITHA ELEMENTS AND TRADITIONS
ACORNS (symbol of fertility and prosperity) ✦ BONFIRES
✦ CANDLES: Blue, green, orange, yellow ✦ CRYSTALS:
Amber, jade, onyx ✦ DEITIES: Apollo, Hestia (Greek); Aten
(Egyptian) ✦ FAERIES ✦ FLOWERS: Carnation, daisy,
sunflower, rose ✦ HERBS: Basil, elderflower, lavender, vervain
✦ HONEY (to celebrate the sun god) ✦ INCENSE: Lemon, rose ✦
TREES: Bay, beech, oak

LAMMAS · July 31 (sunset)–August 1
Lammas (also called Lughnasadh or "loaf mass," or Pagan Thanksgiving) commemorates
the first grain harvest of the year. This is an ancient, celebratory event when the earth's
growth slows and the sun and moon—aka the god and goddess—are bound together,
providing plentiful crops to store throughout the winter months ahead. This time is also about
embracing creativity and harvesting not just food but also memories of your
own personal achievements.

LAMMAS ELEMENTS AND TRADITIONS
CANDLES: Orange, yellow ✦ CORN POPPET (symbol of
good luck and fertility) ✦ CRYSTALS: Agate, carnelian, citrine,
moonstone, peridot ✦ DEITIES: Áine, Cerridwen, and Lugh
(Celtic); Demeter (Greek) ✦ FLOWERS: Sunflower ✦ GRAINS
✦ HERBS: Meadowsweet, mint ✦ INCENSE: Rose, sandalwood ✦
ONION GARLANDS (to absorb negativity) ✦ TREES: Beech,
hawthorn, sycamore

MABON (Autumnal Equinox) · September 20–23
The autumnal equinox falls midway between the harvesting and sowing season. Traditionally,
this festival was about giving thanks to the Welsh god Mabon, said to be the son of the Earth
Mother and the god Modron, although the deities vary by culture. For example, the
Druids paid tribute to the Green Man and gave food offerings to trees, while
Pagans honored the mature goddess as she passed from mother to crone. It is
a time of year to offer thanks and gratitude, and reflect on the past seasons
and the ones to come.

MABON ELEMENTS AND TRADITIONS
CANDLES: green, orange, red, yellow ✦ CORNUCOPIAS (to
represent abundance) ✦ CRYSTALS: Amber, citrine, red aventurine,

peridot ◆ DEITIES: Green Man, Triple Goddess (Pagan); Mabon/Modron (Welsh); Persephone (Greek); Thor (Germanic/Norse) ◆ FLOWERS: Chamomile, honeysuckle, passionflower, rose ◆ FRUITS: apple, pear, plum, pomegranate ◆ HERBS: Saffron, sage, thistle, yarrow ◆ INCENSE: Frankincense, myrrh, sage ◆ TREES: Oak, pine, walnut

SAMHAIN (All Hallow's Eve) • October 31

Samhain, or Sow Wen, is an ancient Gaelic festival and one of the most prominent events in the witch's calendar. Sometimes referred to as All Hallow's Eve, the Feast of the Dead, All Souls' Night, or Halloween, Samhain marks the final chapter of birth and death and makes way for the last harvest of the year. The Sun King is surrendered to the earth, and the crone will grieve him until he is reborn again at Yule. Seeds fall back into the ground and lie lifeless until the cycle once again begins. For witches today, All Hallow's Eve is even more important than Yule, as it is considered to be our new year.

SAMHAIN ELEMENTS AND TRADITIONS

APPLES (to represent immortality) ◆ BROOMSTICKS (to sweep away old energies) ◆ CANDLES: Green, orange, red, yellow ◆ CRYSTALS: Calcite, carnelian, opal, sunstone ◆ DEITIES: Anubis, Osiris (Egyptian); Cerridwen (Celtic); Horned God (Pagan); Hecate, Persephone (Greek); Hel, Odin (Germanic/Norse); Oya (Yoruba) ◆ FLOWERS: All fall flowers ◆ HERBS: Bay, rosemary, vervain ◆ INCENSE: Sandalwood, sweetgrass ◆ PUMPKINS (jack-o'-lanterns) ◆ TREES: Birch, oak, rowan

MAGICKAL MOON PHASES

For thousands of years, the moon has been seen as having a magickal presence, and even our ancestors believed that it had some spiritual significance. There are numerous spells that you can perform during different phases of the moon—certain spells work better during particular phases. All the spells listed on pages 11–12 can be cast in a simple ritual: Take a small white candle to the window and gaze at the moon through the windowpane. Say your wish out loud and with feeling, then leave the candle to burn down (while you are still in the room, of course; do not leave the candle unattended or place it near a curtain).

New Moon ●

New Moons usually cannot be seen with the naked eye. But a day or two after the new moon first appears each month, a slim crescent moon becomes visible. The new moon phase surrounds us with lots of positive energy and can act as a catalyst for immediate change. Many transitions naturally happen around a new moon anyway, such as new jobs, births, and moves, but if you need to revolutionize your life, cast spells at this time for:

Career changes / Moving house swiftly and easily /
Safe and enjoyable travel / Increasing your
cash flow / Better health / Conceiving

Waxing Crescent ● to First Quarter Moon ◐

When the moon is waxing, witches like to cast spells for improving situations or for getting things going if things have been in a rut. Often, when life is unchanging, it takes a little boost to amp things up a bit, and this phase is definitely the best time to kick-start your life. This calendar only includes the first quarter moon symbol, not the waxing crescent. The first quarter moon symbol is shown on the days that the first quarter moon occurs.

The waxing crescent phases occur between the new moon and the first quarter phases. The following spells act faster during a waxing moon:

*Lifting one's mood / Getting out of a rut / Passing examinations
and tests / Finding lost objects / Healing a sick animal or finding a
lost pet / Nurturing abundant, healthy gardens and the
well-being of nature / Losing weight or stopping smoking*

Full Moon ○

From a magickal point of view the full moon does not have any negative connotations; it is just considered a very powerful time of the month. For some reason, Fridays that fall on full moons are wonderful days for casting love spells. There are lots of other spells that benefit from being cast on a full moon, too:

*Protecting your home and property / Adding vigor to your life / Anything to
do with love / Increasing self-confidence /Advancing in career and work /
Enhancing psychic ability / Clairvoyance / Strengthening friendships and family
bonds / Performing general good-luck spells*

Waning Crescent ☽ to Last Quarter Moon ☾

The waning moon is the perfect time to cast spells for getting rid of the black clouds and negative energies that sometimes hang over us. This calendar only includes the last quarter moon symbol, not the waning crescent. The last quarter moon symbol is shown on the days that the last quarter moon occurs. The waning crescent phases occur between the last quarter and the new moon phases. It is a time when you can draw down strength from the universe. If you are surrounded by difficult people and feel you can't cope, or if you have to tackle difficult situations head-on, you can use the moon's power to assist you. By casting spells during this phase, you will gain the power to take control again, strengthen your weak areas, and become more assertive in your actions. Cast spells at this time for:

*Developing inner strength and assertiveness / Banishing enemies /
Stopping arguments / Soothing unruly children / Calming anxiety /
Getting out of tricky situations*

Dark or Void of the Moon

The dark moon, when the face of the moon is hidden, is also known as the "dead" moon. It takes place three days before a new moon and is considered to be the most magickal and potent of all the phases. Sadly, many people who practice black magick do so at this time. You might think that someone working on the darker side of the occult could not influence any spells or rituals that you might be performing, but the collective power mustered by these individuals can cause cosmic havoc: our spells may become confused or simply not work at all. It is a shame, because the brilliance and power of this phase is incredible, and without the negative manipulation I am sure we witches could do a great deal of good in it. Unless you are an experienced wand waver, it is probably best not to attempt any rituals at this time, but to wait until the new moon comes in.

Ritual to Draw Down the Moon

Calling or "drawing down" the moon is a ritual you can perform to engulf yourself within the light of the moon's divine essence. Many witches who cast spells frequently draw on the moon's power before every ritual, while some only do it once a month, usually when the moon is full. We draw down the moon to connect with its powerful rays. You are permitting it to join you in your moment and work its magick alongside you.

Your backyard, a woodland area, or a field are great places to conduct this ceremony. While it is preferable to perform lunar magick outdoors, being indoors or outdoors really doesn't make a lot of difference in the outcome of the spell, because you'll still receive power from the divine light. The important part is being able to see the moon in all its glory. Playing meditative music is also a lovely way to get into the spirit of the spell. You can choose to perform this ritual prior to any spell, only once at the beginning of a new moon phase, or simply when you feel the need for some lunar cleansing. There are many rituals to draw down the moon, but this one should leave you feeling invigorated, cleansed, and in tune with the divine.

Materials
1 (26-ounce) container of salt
A wand or twig*
Chair or stool (optional)

Ritual
Take a fair amount of salt and create a large circle with it on the ground. Step to the side and stand with your legs slightly apart. Point your wand or twig at the moon. Gaze upon the moon's surface and imagine it radiating magick down from the skies. For a few minutes, breathe in its essence and visualize it showering you with magickal beams of light. As you inhale, picture yourself receiving power, and as you exhale, imagine breathing out any impurities in your body. Then say this spell three times:

"I call the goddess of the moon,
Bring your power around me and into my sight,
Silver light, shine down bright this night,
Fill me with your magick soon."

When you have said the spell three times, close it by saying, *"So mote it be."* If you are fit and able, sit cross-legged inside your circle of salt and close your eyes. If not, sit on a chair or stool.

Hold the wand or twig with both hands at each tip, top and bottom, and meditate on it. You might start to feel it become heavy with power or you may feel a tingling sensation run up each arm. If this happens, it's a sign that the moon's magick is transporting its energy toward you. Completely relax your body, letting your head drop to your chin. Feel the stretch at the back of your neck, and hold this position for about ten seconds. Bring the head upward, this time turning it the right. Once again, hold for ten seconds. Repeat this, facing the left. Then, facing straight ahead, push back your shoulders for a further ten seconds before relaxing. Try to stay in this place as long as you can, so the divine light will fully engulf you.

* (Note: Use a fallen twig collected from a nearby tree and be sure to thank the tree for its offering.)

17-MONTH PLANNER

AUGUST 2023

Sunday	Monday	Tuesday	Wednesday
30	31	1 Full Moon ○	2
6	7	8 Last Quarter Moon ◑	9
13	14	15	16 New Moon ●
20	21	22	23
27	28 Summer bank holiday (UK)	29	30 Full Moon ○

Thursday	Friday	Saturday	NOTES
3	4	5	
10	11	12	
17	18	19	
24	25	26	
First Quarter Moon ◑			
31	1	2	

JULY/AUGUST 2023

31 MONDAY

1 TUESDAY

Full Moon ○

2 WEDNESDAY

3 THURSDAY

<table>
<tr><td colspan="7">JULY 2023</td></tr>
<tr><td>S</td><td>M</td><td>T</td><td>W</td><td>T</td><td>F</td><td>S</td></tr>
<tr><td></td><td></td><td></td><td></td><td></td><td></td><td>1</td></tr>
<tr><td>2</td><td>3</td><td>4</td><td>5</td><td>6</td><td>7</td><td>8</td></tr>
<tr><td>9</td><td>10</td><td>11</td><td>12</td><td>13</td><td>14</td><td>15</td></tr>
<tr><td>16</td><td>17</td><td>18</td><td>19</td><td>20</td><td>21</td><td>22</td></tr>
<tr><td>23</td><td>24</td><td>25</td><td>26</td><td>27</td><td>28</td><td>29</td></tr>
<tr><td>30</td><td>31</td><td></td><td></td><td></td><td></td><td></td></tr>
</table>

4 FRIDAY

<table>
<tr><td colspan="7">AUGUST 2023</td></tr>
<tr><td>S</td><td>M</td><td>T</td><td>W</td><td>T</td><td>F</td><td>S</td></tr>
<tr><td></td><td></td><td>1</td><td>2</td><td>3</td><td>4</td><td>5</td></tr>
<tr><td>6</td><td>7</td><td>8</td><td>9</td><td>10</td><td>11</td><td>12</td></tr>
<tr><td>13</td><td>14</td><td>15</td><td>16</td><td>17</td><td>18</td><td>19</td></tr>
<tr><td>20</td><td>21</td><td>22</td><td>23</td><td>24</td><td>25</td><td>26</td></tr>
<tr><td>27</td><td>28</td><td>29</td><td>30</td><td>31</td><td></td><td></td></tr>
</table>

5 SATURDAY

6 SUNDAY

Where to Place Altar Items

Traditionally, a witch's altar should face north, but there are really no hard-and-fast rules: your spells will work just as well wherever you orient your altar. Altar placement is personal to every witch, so you must do what you feel. However, you might want to put your representative objects on the following points of your altar to help your spells along:

North–Earth
CANDLE COLORS: Any shade of green
ITEMS: Pentagrams ✦ salt ✦ dirt from outdoors ✦ metals or ceramics ✦ herbs and flowers ✦ seeds ✦ dried foods ✦ stones or pebbles ✦ crystals

South–Fire
CANDLE COLORS: Red, orange, and brown
ITEMS: Candles ✦ lighters ✦ matches ✦ volcanic stones ✦ spices ✦ orange or yellow flowers ✦ images or figurines of cats, lions, tigers, or dragons

East–Air
CANDLE COLORS: Yellows, cream, and gold
ITEMS: Feathers ✦ athames ✦ swords, knives ✦ wands ✦ wind chimes ✦ bells ✦ incense ✦ anointing oils ✦ images or figurines of angels, fairies, or deities and of birds, dragonflies, or butterflies

West–Water
CANDLE COLORS: Blue, turquoise ✦ white
ITEMS: Chalices ✦ stormwater or rainwater ✦ seashells ✦ crystal ball ✦ mirrors ✦ seaweed ✦ sand ✦ wine (white, red, or rosé) ✦ images or figurines of mermaids, fish, dolphins, or whales

AUGUST 2023

7 MONDAY

8 TUESDAY

Last Quarter Moon

9 WEDNESDAY

10 THURSDAY

AUGUST 2023						
S	M	T	W	T	F	S
		1	2	3	4	5
6	7	8	9	10	11	12
13	14	15	16	17	18	19
20	21	22	23	24	25	26
27	28	29	30	31		

11 FRIDAY

SEPTEMBER 2023						
S	M	T	W	T	F	S
					1	2
3	4	5	6	7	8	9
10	11	12	13	14	15	16
17	18	19	20	21	22	23
24	25	26	27	28	29	30

12 SATURDAY

13 SUNDAY

14 MONDAY

15 TUESDAY

16 WEDNESDAY

New Moon ●

17 THURSDAY

18 FRIDAY

19 SATURDAY

20 SUNDAY

AUGUST 2023

21 MONDAY

22 TUESDAY

23 WEDNESDAY

24 THURSDAY

First Quarter Moon ◑

25 FRIDAY

26 SATURDAY

27 SUNDAY

A Spell for Feeling Energized

Most of us lead hectic lives that become may become even busier as summer winds down and fall begins; burnout can leave us feeling sluggish and lethargic. Bloodstone possesses magickal properties that boost energy and leave us feeling invigorated.

Materials

    A polished bloodstone

    An oak leaf, for strength

    A votive or tealight candle, in red

Ritual

Cleanse and empower your stone (see pages 170–71). Venture outdoors during any moon phase and find an oak tree. Hold your bloodstone against the bark of the tree and ask it to help you feel more energized and motivated. Take one leaf from the tree, being sure to thank it. Back at home, set up an altar. Place your stone on top of the leaf and light the candle. Say the following mantra twelve times:

> *"Energy and drive will be my prize,*
> *My body, my soul, I sanitize."*

After you've recited the spell twelve times, close it by adding *"So mote it be."* Leave everything in situ on the altar until the candle has burned down. Place the leaf inside your shoe for at least a week and sleep with the stone nearby at night.

AUGUST/SEPTEMBER 2023

28 MONDAY

Summer bank holiday (UK)

29 TUESDAY

30 WEDNESDAY

Full Moon ○

31 THURSDAY

AUGUST 2023						
S	M	T	W	T	F	S
		1	2	3	4	5
6	7	8	9	10	11	12
13	14	15	16	17	18	19
20	21	22	23	24	25	26
27	28	29	30	31		

1 FRIDAY

SEPTEMBER 2023						
S	M	T	W	T	F	S
					1	2
3	4	5	6	7	8	9
10	11	12	13	14	15	16
17	18	19	20	21	22	23
24	25	26	27	28	29	30

2 SATURDAY

3 SUNDAY

SEPTEMBER 2023

Sunday	Monday	Tuesday	Wednesday
27	28	29	30
3	4 Labor Day (US, CAN)	5	6 Last Quarter Moon
10	11	12	13
17	18	19	20
24 Yom Kippur (begins at sundown)	25	26	27

Thursday	Friday	Saturday	NOTES
31	1	2	
7	8	9	
14 New Moon ●	15 Rosh Hashanah (begins at sundown)	16	
21	22 Mabon (Autumnal Equinox) First Quarter Moon ◗	23	
28	29 Full Moon ○	30	

SEPTEMBER 2023

4 MONDAY

Labor Day (US, CAN)

5 TUESDAY

6 WEDNESDAY

Last Quarter Moon ◑

7 THURSDAY

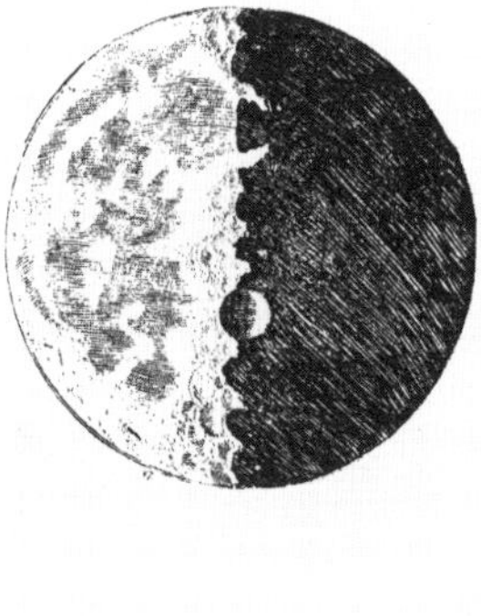

8 FRIDAY

9 SATURDAY

10 SUNDAY

SEPTEMBER 2023

11 MONDAY

12 TUESDAY

13 WEDNESDAY

14 THURSDAY

New Moon ●

15 FRIDAY

Rosh Hashanah (begins at sundown)

16 SATURDAY

17 SUNDAY

SEPTEMBER 2023						
S	M	T	W	T	F	S
					1	2
3	4	5	6	7	8	9
10	11	12	13	14	15	16
17	18	19	20	21	22	23
24	25	26	27	28	29	30

OCTOBER 2023						
S	M	T	W	T	F	S
1	2	3	4	5	6	7
8	9	10	11	12	13	14
15	16	17	18	19	20	21
22	23	24	25	26	27	28
29	30	31				

MABON
(AUTUMNAL EQUINOX)
September 20–23

Now, as the year begins to wane, it is time to quietly reflect and look back over the past months. This is the second harvest, the autumnal equinox, a thoughtful time when our ancestors accumulated the harvest they had labored so hard to produce. In modern Wicca, we see Mabon as a period of contemplation, but we also use it as a time to clear out any clutter and recycle things we no longer need. The expression "Tidy house, tidy mind" is the focus here. Creating order surrounded by neatness and harmony in life brings a sense of pleasure and contentment.

Mabon is a perfect time to celebrate the humble apple. When you cut an apple in half widthwise, you will see the sign of a pentagram. If you cut it in half down its length, the symbol inside is of the female genitalia. Because of their magickal significance, apples are often present on the altar during Mabon festivals.

SEPTEMBER 2023

18 MONDAY

19 TUESDAY

20 WEDNESDAY

21 THURSDAY

SEPTEMBER 2023

S	M	T	W	T	F	S
					1	2
3	4	5	6	7	8	9
10	11	12	13	14	15	16
17	18	19	20	21	22	23
24	25	26	27	28	29	30

22 FRIDAY

Mabon (Autumnal Equinox)
First Quarter Moon ◑

OCTOBER 2023

S	M	T	W	T	F	S
1	2	3	4	5	6	7
8	9	10	11	12	13	14
15	16	17	18	19	20	21
22	23	24	25	26	27	28
29	30	31				

23 SATURDAY

24 SUNDAY

Yom Kippur
(begins at sundown)

25 MONDAY

26 TUESDAY

27 WEDNESDAY

28 THURSDAY

29 FRIDAY

Full Moon ◯

30 SATURDAY

1 SUNDAY

SEPTEMBER 2023						
S	M	T	W	T	F	S
					1	2
3	4	5	6	7	8	9
10	11	12	13	14	15	16
17	18	19	20	21	22	23
24	25	26	27	28	29	30

OCTOBER 2023						
S	M	T	W	T	F	S
1	2	3	4	5	6	7
8	9	10	11	12	13	14
15	16	17	18	19	20	21
22	23	24	25	26	27	28
29	30	31				

OCTOBER 2023

Sunday	Monday	Tuesday	Wednesday
1	2	3	4
8	9 Indigenous Peoples' Day, Columbus Day (US), Thanksgiving (CAN)	10	11
15	16	17	18
22	23	24	25
29	30	31 Samhain, Halloween	1

Thursday	Friday	Saturday
5	6	7
	Last Quarter Moon ◐	
12	13	14
		New Moon ●
19	20	21
		First Quarter Moon ◑
26	27	28
		Full Moon ○
2	3	4

OCTOBER 2023

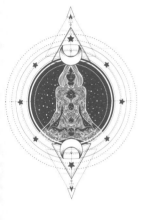

2 MONDAY

3 TUESDAY

4 WEDNESDAY

5 THURSDAY

OCTOBER 2023

S	M	T	W	T	F	S
1	2	3	4	5	6	7
8	9	10	11	12	13	14
15	16	17	18	19	20	21
22	23	24	25	26	27	28
29	30	31				

6 FRIDAY

Last Quarter Moon ◑

NOVEMBER 2023

S	M	T	W	T	F	S
			1	2	3	4
5	6	7	8	9	10	11
12	13	14	15	16	17	18
19	20	21	22	23	24	25
26	27	28	29	30		

7 SATURDAY

8 SUNDAY

9 MONDAY

Indigenous People's Day,
Columbus Day (US),
Thanksgiving (CAN)

10 TUESDAY

11 WEDNESDAY

12 THURSDAY

OCTOBER 2023						
S	M	T	W	T	F	S
1	2	3	4	5	6	7
8	9	10	11	12	13	14
15	16	17	18	19	20	21
22	23	24	25	26	27	28
29	30	31				

13 FRIDAY

NOVEMBER 2023						
S	M	T	W	T	F	S
			1	2	3	4
5	6	7	8	9	10	11
12	13	14	15	16	17	18
19	20	21	22	23	24	25
26	27	28	29	30		

14 SATURDAY

15 SUNDAY

New Moon ●

Sleep-Well Spell

There are times in life when you want to bring the energy down a notch, particularly if you need a good night's sleep. Here is a ritual that will help.

Materials

> Vanilla-scented candle
> Handful of Epsom salts
> 6–8 drops lavender essential oil*

Ritual

Light the vanilla-scented candle and place it in your bathroom. Fill your bathtub and sprinkle in a handful of Epsom salts and 6–8 drops of lavender essential oil. Inhale deeply and say:

> *"Restful slumber come to me,*
> *Let my mind sleep peacefully."*

Repeat this as you soak for 15–20 minutes, practicing deep breathing. Stressful thoughts may enter your mind. Let them linger for a moment, but then visualize yourself placing them into a beautiful container and putting a lid on it tightly. Imagine handing this container off to your higher power or mentally stow it away in a closet to deal with in the morning.

When you are finished, rinse off with clean water to wash away any lingering negative or overactive energy. Blow out the candle. As you climb into bed, continue the pattern of deep breathing and your restful sleep chant. Imagine all of the things you are grateful for. Let tomorrow's worries come to you during daylight hours when they are less likely to seem overwhelming.

*Note: Other essential oils you can substitute for lavender oil include cedarwood, chamomile, frankincense, valerian, vetiver, and ylang-ylang. It is best to do a 24-hour patch test on a small area of skin before using any essential oil.

16 MONDAY

17 TUESDAY

18 WEDNESDAY

19 THURSDAY

20 FRIDAY

21 SATURDAY

22 SUNDAY

First Quarter Moon ◑

OCTOBER 2023

23 MONDAY

24 TUESDAY

25 WEDNESDAY

26 THURSDAY

OCTOBER 2023

S	M	T	W	T	F	S
1	2	3	4	5	6	7
8	9	10	11	12	13	14
15	16	17	18	19	20	21
22	23	24	25	26	27	28
29	30	31				

27 FRIDAY

NOVEMBER 2023

S	M	T	W	T	F	S
			1	2	3	4
5	6	7	8	9	10	11
12	13	14	15	16	17	18
19	20	21	22	23	24	25
26	27	28	29	30		

28 SATURDAY

Full Moon ○

29 SUNDAY

SAMHAIN
(ALL HALLOW'S EVE)
October 31

Samhain or All Hallow's Eve marks the witch's new year. From a magickal point of view, it is a time when the veil separating the spirit world from the earth is lifted, meaning we can communicate with the dead and lost loved ones. Centuries ago, people would dress up in scary costumes to frighten away evil spirits that might walk through the veil. It is an incredibly powerful time when magick amplifies, divination intensifies, and spells and rituals become more potent. A favorite tradition is to cast a spell for each family member. Write down their need on paper and light them a candle during the evening of Samhain. Then say the following words for every member:

"Powers climb into the night, with this candle that I light,
Wishes granted with what I write, magick comes with joyful light.
So mote it be."

There is also no better time than Samhain to have a party, but a witch's gathering is not of the usual ghostly, ghoulish variety. Invite friends and family to feast on pumpkin soup, breads, seasonal meats, and vegetables. Cast spells for the good of mankind (and maybe drink a little too much homemade wine).

OCTOBER/NOVEMBER 2023

30 MONDAY

31 TUESDAY

Samhain
Halloween

1 WEDNESDAY

2 THURSDAY

OCTOBER 2023						
S	M	T	W	T	F	S
1	2	3	4	5	6	7
8	9	10	11	12	13	14
15	16	17	18	19	20	21
22	23	24	25	26	27	28
29	30	31				

3 FRIDAY

NOVEMBER 2023						
S	M	T	W	T	F	S
			1	2	3	4
5	6	7	8	9	10	11
12	13	14	15	16	17	18
19	20	21	22	23	24	25
26	27	28	29	30		

4 SATURDAY

5 SUNDAY

Daylight Saving Time Ends
(US, CAN)
Last Quarter Moon ◐

NOVEMBER 2023

Sunday	Monday	Tuesday	Wednesday
29	30	31	1
5 Daylight Saving Time Ends (US, CAN)	6	7 Election Day (US)	8
12	13 New Moon ●	14	15
19	20 First Quarter Moon ◐	21	22
26	27 Full Moon ○	28	29

Thursday	Friday	Saturday	NOTES
2	3	4	
9	10	11 Veterans Day (US)	
16	17	18	
23	24	25	
30	1	2	

NOVEMBER 2023

6 MONDAY

---

7 TUESDAY

Election Day

8 WEDNESDAY

---

9 THURSDAY

10 FRIDAY

11 SATURDAY

12 SUNDAY

Veterans Day

13 MONDAY

New Moon ●

14 TUESDAY

15 WEDNESDAY

16 THURSDAY

NOVEMBER 2023						
S	M	T	W	T	F	S
			1	2	3	4
5	6	7	8	9	10	11
12	13	14	15	16	17	18
19	20	21	22	23	24	25
26	27	28	29	30		

17 FRIDAY

18 SATURDAY

19 SUNDAY

DECEMBER 2023						
S	M	T	W	T	F	S
					1	2
3	4	5	6	7	8	9
10	11	12	13	14	15	16
17	18	19	20	21	22	23
24	25	26	27	28	29	30
31						

Mystical Crystal Gratitude Ritual

We all tend to take certain things for granted, which is exactly why it's important to stop and think about all that we have and are able to enjoy. Take some time to think about your life, your accomplishments, your goals, your abilities, and the things you've overcome. Make your own gratitude list and celebrate it into a ritual of thanks.

You can always incorporate mystical elements into your thanksgiving ritual, like the following:

- White candles are used to promote peace and harmony and represent the unity of spirits.

- Other candles represent (quite literally) light shining through the darkness.

- An angelite crystal or pendant boosts the spirit and gives strength to your intention.

- Amethyst chases away anxiety, fear, and sadness. Negative energies don't stand a chance when amethyst is on the scene!

- Rose quartz is the stone of universal love and acceptance. This is a perfect stone to use if you've had a major life change and you're searching for the positive aspects of your new situation. It also promotes spiritual healing and inner peace.

- Add some aromatherapy. Lavender promotes relaxation. Frankincense improves concentration. Citrus oils lighten the mood.

20 MONDAY

First Quarter Moon 🌓

21 TUESDAY

22 WEDNESDAY

23 THURSDAY

Thanksgiving (US)

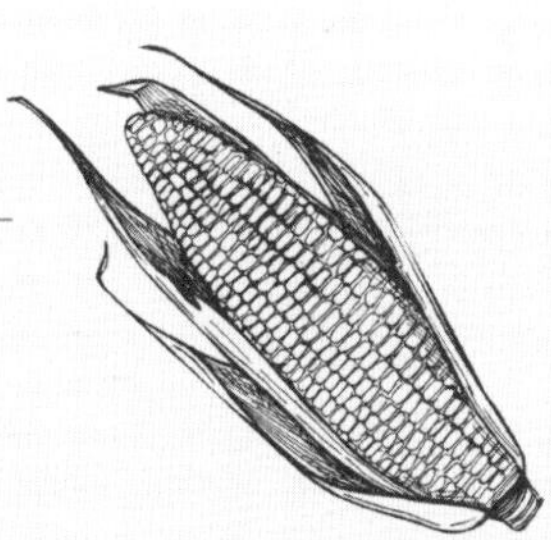

24 FRIDAY

25 SATURDAY

26 SUNDAY

NOVEMBER/DECEMBER 2023

27 MONDAY

Full Moon ◯

28 TUESDAY

29 WEDNESDAY

30 THURSDAY

NOVEMBER 2023

S	M	T	W	T	F	S
			1	2	3	4
5	6	7	8	9	10	11
12	13	14	15	16	17	18
19	20	21	22	23	24	25
26	27	28	29	30		

1 FRIDAY

DECEMBER 2023

S	M	T	W	T	F	S
					1	2
3	4	5	6	7	8	9
10	11	12	13	14	15	16
17	18	19	20	21	22	23
24	25	26	27	28	29	30
31						

2 SATURDAY

3 SUNDAY

DECEMBER 2023

Sunday	Monday	Tuesday	Wednesday
26	27	28	29
3	4	5 Last Quarter Moon ◑	6
10	11	12 New Moon ●	13
17	18	19 First Quarter Moon ◐	20
24	25 Christmas Day	26 Kwanzaa, Boxing Day (CAN) Full Moon ○	27
31 New Year's Eve	1	2	3

Thursday	Friday	Saturday	NOTES
30	1	2	
7 Hanukkah (begins at sundown)	8	9	
14	15	16	
21 Yule (Winter Solstice)	22	23	
28	29	30	
4	5	6	

A Spell to Protect Wildlife in Winter

During harsh winters, birds and other wildlife often perish. It's important for a witch to help them not just survive in these cold months—no matter where you live—but to thrive.

Materials

- 3 candles, in green, brown, and blue, for representation of nature's colors
- 3 lengths of ribbon, in green, brown, and blue

Ritual

Stand the three different-colored candles in the center of your workplace, in any order. Light them.

Take the three lengths of ribbon and knot them together at the top before braiding them into a plait. Fasten the plait at the bottom. Lay the braid in front of the candles and say this spell three times:

> *"Goddess of wildlife, discharge your power,*
> *Bring safety and contentment, hour upon hour,*
> *Treasure the animals who reside outside,*
> *Be their comfort, be their guide."*

When you have said the spell three times, close it by adding, "So mote it be."

Let the candles burn down (do not leave them unattended). When they have extinguished themselves, go outside and tie the braid to a branch of any tree in your yard or on your street. If you have a yard or garden, feed the birds and put out fresh water when the thermometer drops and make sure that if it freezes you break up or melt the ice so that the birds always have a drink. (We pour warm water on our icy bird baths in freezing conditions.)

DECEMBER 2023

4 MONDAY

5 TUESDAY

Last Quarter Moon

6 WEDNESDAY

7 THURSDAY

DECEMBER 2023						
S	M	T	W	T	F	S
					1	2
3	4	5	6	7	8	9
10	11	12	13	14	15	16
17	18	19	20	21	22	23
24	25	26	27	28	29	30
31						

Hanukkah (begins at sundown)

8 FRIDAY

JANUARY 2024						
S	M	T	W	T	F	S
	1	2	3	4	5	6
7	8	9	10	11	12	13
14	15	16	17	18	19	20
21	22	23	24	25	26	27
28	29	30	31			

9 SATURDAY

10 SUNDAY

11 MONDAY

12 TUESDAY

New Moon ●

13 WEDNESDAY

14 THURSDAY

DECEMBER 2023

S	M	T	W	T	F	S
					1	2
3	4	5	6	7	8	9
10	11	12	13	14	15	16
17	18	19	20	21	22	23
24	25	26	27	28	29	30
31						

15 FRIDAY

16 SATURDAY

17 SUNDAY

JANUARY 2024

S	M	T	W	T	F	S
	1	2	3	4	5	6
7	8	9	10	11	12	13
14	15	16	17	18	19	20
21	22	23	24	25	26	27
28	29	30	31			

YULE
(WINTER SOLSTICE)
December 20–23

The Feast of Juul was celebrated by the ancient Germanic people and lasted twelve days, during which they would grieve the death of the old god and honor the goddess while she gave birth to the new Sun King. In commemoration, they would burn a Yule or Juul log lit from a small part of the previous year's tree, to ensure good luck.

These traditions traveled around Europe: the French cut up the log and brought a small amount inside to burn each day. In Cornwall, England, the Cornish would remove all bark before burning. In some parts of the United Kingdom, they replaced the log with ash twigs or candles. Nowadays, we evoke Yule logs by enjoying Swiss roll cakes covered in chocolate and delighting in the pleasures of indulgence. People celebrated Yuletide not only by feasting but also by giving gifts of food to neighbors and friends. This may be where the tradition of gift-giving during Christmas was born.

THE YULE LOG

DECEMBER 2023

18 MONDAY

19 TUESDAY

First Quarter Moon ◑

20 WEDNESDAY

21 THURSDAY

Yule (Winter Solstice)

22 FRIDAY

DECEMBER 2023						
S	M	T	W	T	F	S
					1	2
3	4	5	6	7	8	9
10	11	12	13	14	15	16
17	18	19	20	21	22	23
24	25	26	27	28	29	30
31						

JANUARY 2024						
S	M	T	W	T	F	S
	1	2	3	4	5	6
7	8	9	10	11	12	13
14	15	16	17	18	19	20
21	22	23	24	25	26	27
28	29	30	31			

23 SATURDAY

24 SUNDAY

Light Energy Magick

Quantum mechanics is a theory concerning atomic and subatomic particles in physics. It states that, when viewed at the subatomic level, particles don't behave the way we would otherwise expect them to.

Light is energy, and we are all made of energy and surrounded by energy, which can also be manipulated by certain forces, including our consciousness and our intention. This is pretty heady stuff, but what it means for us is that we can manipulate forces by focusing on what we want to bring about. This is the definition of magick, after all, and when we talk about meditation or the use of crystals, chants, or music in spellcasting, this is what we're doing: affecting the forces and energies that are already surrounding us.

Try these fun and easy experiments:

- During meditation, send love to someone who has been unlovable lately.

- Focus on something you want to materialize. Believe it has already happened.

- Create a policy of all-positive thoughts for 24 hours. If you hear negative news, try to find a silver lining. See what happens.

Remember that we are all part of one unified energy, and we all have a part in the form it takes. Let's each do our best to make it as beautiful, prosperous, and light as possible.

DECEMBER 2023

25 MONDAY

Christmas Day

26 TUESDAY

Kwanzaa, Boxing Day (UK, CAN)
Full Moon ◯

27 WEDNESDAY

28 THURSDAY

DECEMBER 2023

S	M	T	W	T	F	S
					1	2
3	4	5	6	7	8	9
10	11	12	13	14	15	16
17	18	19	20	21	22	23
24	25	26	27	28	29	30
31						

29 FRIDAY

JANUARY 2024

S	M	T	W	T	F	S
	1	2	3	4	5	6
7	8	9	10	11	12	13
14	15	16	17	18	19	20
21	22	23	24	25	26	27
28	29	30	31			

30 SATURDAY

31 SUNDAY

New Year's Eve

JANUARY 2024

Sunday	Monday	Tuesday	Wednesday
30	1 New Year's Day	2	3 Last Quarter Moon
7	8	9	10
14	15 Martin Luther King Jr. Day	16	17 First Quarter Moon
21	22	23	24
28	29	30	31

Thursday	Friday	Saturday
4	5	6
11	12	13
New Moon ●		
18	19	20
25	26	27
Full Moon ○	Australia Day	
1	2	3

1 MONDAY

New Year's Day

2 TUESDAY

3 WEDNESDAY

Last Quarter Moon ◗

4 THURSDAY

5 FRIDAY

6 SATURDAY

7 SUNDAY

JANUARY 2024

8 MONDAY

9 TUESDAY

10 WEDNESDAY

11 THURSDAY

New Moon ●

12 FRIDAY

13 SATURDAY

14 SUNDAY

15 MONDAY

Martin Luther King Jr. Day

16 TUESDAY

17 WEDNESDAY

First Quarter Moon ◗

18 THURSDAY

19 FRIDAY

20 SATURDAY

21 SUNDAY

JANUARY 2024

22 MONDAY

23 TUESDAY

24 WEDNESDAY

25 THURSDAY

JANUARY 2024						
S	M	T	W	T	F	S
	1	2	3	4	5	6
7	8	9	10	11	12	13
14	15	16	17	18	19	20
21	22	23	24	25	26	27
28	29	30	31			

Full Moon ◯

26 FRIDAY

Australia Day

FEBRUARY 2024						
S	M	T	W	T	F	S
				1	2	3
4	5	6	7	8	9	10
11	12	13	14	15	16	17
18	19	20	21	22	23	24
25	26	27	28	29		

27 SATURDAY

28 SUNDAY

IMBOLC

February 2

The holiday honors the Celtic triple goddess Brigid, who generates fertility to the land and its individuals and is especially connected to birth. The soil is stirring, seeds are starting to sprout, and the cold, dark days of winter are at last in the past.

Spells and rituals for fertility and abundance are cast at this time, and this period inspires a thorough spring-clean, clearing away the old and making way for the new. Imbolc is also a fire pageant, symbolic of the sun soon returning to warm the earth.

February 1–2 are magickal days to plant seeds or flowers that will later bloom when the weather warms up. When you have finished planting your seeds in the ground, stand over the soil and make a silent wish for the coming season.

JANUARY/FEBRUARY 2024

29 MONDAY

30 TUESDAY

31 WEDNESDAY

1 THURSDAY

2 FRIDAY

Imbolc

Groundhog Day

Last Quarter Moon ◑

3 SATURDAY

4 SUNDAY

FEBRUARY 2024

Sunday	Monday	Tuesday	Wednesday
28	29	30	31
4	5	6	7
11	12	13	14 Valentine's Day Ash Wednesday
18	19 Presidents' Day	20	21
25	26	27	28

Thursday	Friday	Saturday	NOTES
1	2	3	
	Imbolc Groundhog Day Last Quarter Moon ◑		
8	9	10	
	New Moon ●	Lunar New Year (Year of the Dragon)	
15	16	17	
	First Quarter Moon ◐		
22	23	24	
		Full Moon ○	
29	1	2	
Leap Day			

FEBRUARY 2024

5 MONDAY

6 TUESDAY

7 WEDNESDAY

8 THURSDAY

9 FRIDAY

New Moon ●

10 SATURDAY

Lunar New Year
(Year of the Dragon)

11 SUNDAY

FEBRUARY 2024

12 MONDAY

13 TUESDAY

14 WEDNESDAY

Valentine's Day
Ash Wednesday

15 THURSDAY

FEBRUARY 2024						
S	M	T	W	T	F	S
				1	2	3
4	5	6	7	8	9	10
11	12	13	14	15	16	17
18	19	20	21	22	23	24
25	26	27	28	29		

16 FRIDAY

First Quarter Moon ◑

MARCH 2024						
S	M	T	W	T	F	S
					1	2
3	4	5	6	7	8	9
10	11	12	13	14	15	16
17	18	19	20	21	22	23
24	25	26	27	28	29	30
31						

17 SATURDAY

18 SUNDAY

A Spell to Bring Love into Your Life

When casting spells relating to love, if possible, try beginning or repeating the ritual on a Friday during a full moon phase. Traditionally this is when the moon's energy is perfect for love magick, so you will have more success.

Materials

- 1 pink candle (to represent love)
  Pen and piece of paper
- 1 small white piece of cloth or a handkerchief
- 1 small heart cut from a piece of cardstock

- Scissors
- 1 pink ribbon, for love
  Your favorite perfume

Ritual

Place all the items on your altar, with the candle in the center. Light it. Write your name on the piece of paper and then, using as many words as you like, describe the kind of partner you want. This is your wish list, so be as creative as you like. Place the list in the middle of the cloth or handkerchief—fold the paper if necessary—and lay the cut-out heart on top. Say this spell seven times:

> *"I desire for my blessings to thrive, with this spell, romance is alive,*
> *With no earthly binds, my heart is free,*
> *I summon my cupid to bring love to me."*

When you have finished reciting the spell seven times, close it by adding, *"So mote it be."* Snip a small lock of your hair with the scissors and position it on the cut-out heart. Bring all four corners of the cloth together and secure it with the pink ribbon. Lastly, squirt the pouch with perfume and leave it near the lit candle until the candle burns out (supervised, of course). Once the flame extinguishes itself, move the pouch into your pocket or purse. Carry it for a few weeks.

19 MONDAY

Presidents' Day

20 TUESDAY

21 WEDNESDAY

22 THURSDAY

23 FRIDAY

24 SATURDAY | **25** SUNDAY

Full Moon ◯

FEBRUARY/MARCH 2024

26 MONDAY

27 TUESDAY

28 WEDNESDAY

29 THURSDAY

Leap Day

1 FRIDAY

2 SATURDAY

3 SUNDAY

Last Quarter Moon ◑

MARCH 2024

Sunday	Monday	Tuesday	Wednesday
26	27	28	29
3 Last Quarter Moon ◑	4	5	6
10 Daylight Saving Time Begins (US, CAN) Ramadan (begins at sundown) New Moon ●	11 Commonwealth Day (UK, CAN, AUS, NZ)	12	13
17 St. Patrick's Day First Quarter Moon ◐	18	19 Ostara (Spring Equinox)	20
24 Palm Sunday	25 Full Moon ○	26	27
31 Easter	1	2	3

Thursday	Friday	Saturday
30	1	2
7	8	9
14	15	16
21	22	23
28	29 Good Friday	30
4	5	6

4 MONDAY

5 TUESDAY

6 WEDNESDAY

7 THURSDAY

8 FRIDAY

9 SATURDAY

10 SUNDAY
Daylight Saving Time Begins
(US, CAN)
Ramadan (begins at sundown)
New Moon ●

MARCH 2024

11 MONDAY

Commonwealth Day (UK, CAN, AUS, NZ)

12 TUESDAY

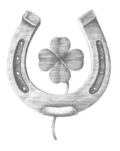

13 WEDNESDAY

14 THURSDAY

MARCH 2024						
S	M	T	W	T	F	S
					1	2
3	4	5	6	7	8	9
10	11	12	13	14	15	16
17	18	19	20	21	22	23
24	25	26	27	28	29	30
31						

15 FRIDAY

APRIL 2024						
S	M	T	W	T	F	S
	1	2	3	4	5	6
7	8	9	10	11	12	13
14	15	16	17	18	19	20
21	22	23	24	25	26	27
28	29	30				

16 SATURDAY

17 SUNDAY

St. Patrick's Day
First Quarter Moon ◗

OSTARA
(SPRING EQUINOX)
March 19–23

During the spring equinox—also known as the vernal equinox in the Northern Hemisphere and the autumnal equinox in the Southern Hemisphere—the sun is directly above the equator at noon, and there are nearly equal hours of day and night at all latitudes. It is also ushers in the Sabbat of Ostara in honor of the Germanic goddess of the dawn Éostre, who symbolizes spring and fertility, prosperity and growth.

Villagers celebrated by planting crops. Witches cast spells to shake off bad luck, leaving a positive and motivated frame of mind. Many witches also use this time to rejoice in the well-being of women and fertility. We call upon Ostara to help us become more independent, self-sufficient, and successful in the coming year. The Ostara Sabbat is also is a perfect backdrop for rituals that change one's luck from bad to good, for healing and health, and for removing blocks and obstacles. See the spell on page 87 for one to try.

MARCH 2024

18 MONDAY

19 TUESDAY

Ostara (Spring Equinox)

20 WEDNESDAY

21 THURSDAY

MARCH 2024						
S	M	T	W	T	F	S
					1	2
3	4	5	6	7	8	9
10	11	12	13	14	15	16
17	18	19	20	21	22	23
24	25	26	27	28	29	30
31						

22 FRIDAY

APRIL 2024						
S	M	T	W	T	F	S
	1	2	3	4	5	6
7	8	9	10	11	12	13
14	15	16	17	18	19	20
21	22	23	24	25	26	27
28	29	30				

23 SATURDAY

24 SUNDAY

Palm Sunday

25 MONDAY

Full Moon ○

26 TUESDAY

27 WEDNESDAY

28 THURSDAY

29 FRIDAY

Good Friday

30 SATURDAY

31 SUNDAY

Easter

MARCH 2024						
S	M	T	W	T	F	S
					1	2
3	4	5	6	7	8	9
10	11	12	13	14	15	16
17	18	19	20	21	22	23
24	25	26	27	28	29	30
31						

APRIL 2024						
S	M	T	W	T	F	S
	1	2	3	4	5	6
7	8	9	10	11	12	13
14	15	16	17	18	19	20
21	22	23	24	25	26	27
28	29	30				

An Ostara Spell for Removing Obstacles

If you or someone you know is at a standstill in life or if you simply want to safeguard yourself against obstacles, this spell will thwart any negative energy, giving you and your aura a thorough spring-clean. It is best performed on the spring equinox.

Materials

- 1 single spring flower, such as daffodil, crocus, or violet
- 1 candle, in pale green, purple, or yellow
- Hot cross buns
- 1 medium bowl
- Bark or twigs, from ash, alder, or birch
- Hare ornament, to represent Ostara (optional)
- 1 amazonite stone

Ritual

Set up your altar and place the spring flower in the center. Take the candle and light it next to the flower. Place a few hot cross buns in the bowl and set the bowl next to the candle. To the altar add some bark, twigs, or even a hare ornament. While the candle burns, empower a piece of amazonite (see pages 170–71) with intent. Visualize yourself running through a spring meadow, as free as a bird, stopping every now and again to smell the flowers. After a few minutes of this, rest the stone directly in front of the candle and say the following incantation three times:

> *"This Ostara I cleanse my space, removing blocks from every place,*
> *Peace in my heart and calmness of mind, an easy path ahead I'll find."*

After you've recited the spell three times, close it by adding *"So mote it be."* While the candle is burning, hold the amazonite in one hand and eat one of the buns with the other. Allow the candle to burn down. You could give the remaining buns to family members so that they can also receive the magickal blessing. When the candle has burned down (attended), press the flower in a heavy book for a week or so. Save this flower for any other spells you might want to cast during the spring months. Keep the stone at home in a safe place for the foreseeable future. Don't throw away any other altar items; just keep them in a safe place to use later.

APRIL 2024

Sunday	Monday	Tuesday	Wednesday
31	1 Easter Monday (UK) Last Quarter Moon ◑	2	3
7	8 New Moon ●	9 Eid al-Fitr (begins at sundown)	10
14	15 First Quarter Moon ◐	16	17
21	22 Earth Day Passover (begins at sundown)	23 Full Moon ○	24
28	29	30	1

Thursday	Friday	Saturday	NOTES
4	5	6	
11	12	13	
18	19	20	
25 Anzac Day (AUS, NZ)	26	27	
2	3	4	

APRIL 2024

1 MONDAY

Easter Monday (UK)
Last Quarter Moon

2 TUESDAY

3 WEDNESDAY

4 THURSDAY

APRIL 2024						
S	M	T	W	T	F	S
	1	2	3	4	5	6
7	8	9	10	11	12	13
14	15	16	17	18	19	20
21	22	23	24	25	26	27
28	29	30				

5 FRIDAY

MAY 2024						
S	M	T	W	T	F	S
			1	2	3	4
5	6	7	8	9	10	11
12	13	14	15	16	17	18
19	20	21	22	23	24	25
26	27	28	29	30	31	

6 SATURDAY

7 SUNDAY

22

APRIL 2024

8 MONDAY

New Moon ●

9 TUESDAY

Eid al-Fitr (begins at sundown)

10 WEDNESDAY

11 THURSDAY

12 FRIDAY

13 SATURDAY

14 SUNDAY

92

APRIL 2024

15 MONDAY

First Quarter Moon ◑

16 TUESDAY

17 WEDNESDAY

18 THURSDAY

19 FRIDAY

20 SATURDAY

21 SUNDAY

A Spell for Healing the Earth

Using crystal craft is a powerful way to help heal the environment, though the success of your spell might come about in strange ways. The spell could radiate toward people with the power to change laws, shifting their mind-set and motivating them into action. Of course, if all the world's leaders start banding together to end pollution, there will be no proof that it was your spell's doing. But if we all pull together and try, our collective energy could really make a difference. This spell needs to be cast twice a year on the morning of a new moon phase.

Materials

7 small, clear quartz crystals
  Large altar or pillar candle
  Small bowl of soil
  Dish of rainwater

Ritual

Cleanse and empower your crystals (see pages pages 170–71). While empowering them, visualize a perfect planet. Imagine marine life swimming in clear blue oceans and envisage large companies recycling plastic items and politicians joining together, discussing the environment. Position your seven crystals in a circle on your altar with the candle in the center, and the soil and water placed inside the crystal ring. Light the candle and recite this spell twelve times:

> *"Protect this planet and all that reside,*
> *animals and humans to stand side by side,*
> *Bring all into balance and heal with your light,*
> *bathe it in beauty in day and at night."*

After you've recited the spell twelve times, close it by adding *"So mote it be."* Let the candle burn for an hour, then blow it out. Take the crystals outside and push them into the ground. Each night light the candle and recite the spell just once. After an hour, blow it out again. Repeat this every night until the candle has burned all the way down.

APRIL 2024

22 MONDAY

Earth Day
Passover (begins at sundown)

23 TUESDAY

Full Moon ○

24 WEDNESDAY

25 THURSDAY

Anzac Day (AUS, NZ)

26 FRIDAY

APRIL 2024

S	M	T	W	T	F	S
	1	2	3	4	5	6
7	8	9	10	11	12	13
14	15	16	17	18	19	20
21	22	23	24	25	26	27
28	29	30				

MAY 2024

S	M	T	W	T	F	S
			1	2	3	4
5	6	7	8	9	10	11
12	13	14	15	16	17	18
19	20	21	22	23	24	25
26	27	28	29	30	31	

27 SATURDAY

28 SUNDAY

BELTANE
(MAY DAY)

April 30–May 1

Beltane is the May Day Gaelic fire festival, welcoming the start of the summer farming season. It was traditionally commemorated by lighting bonfires, then driving cattle around the fires to bless them in the months ahead. Any hearth fires would be extinguished at Beltane and a new one lit. It is a joyous Sabbat where sexuality, love, and fertility are celebrated. When it comes to conception, it is believed that making love outside, under the stars (and in a private place), will ripen your chances of fertility.

The maypole was part of European folk festivals, and on May Day people attached ribbons and cords to a tree and danced around it. It's not the easiest of tasks to create a full-size maypole in the garden, but if you wanted to have a Beltane party, it would be a great centerpiece. Nowadays witches like to make miniature maypoles to place on the altar. They do this by sourcing a dowel rod about 2 feet (60 cm) in length, securing it to a wooden circular base, and gluing or attaching ribbons to the top.

APRIL/MAY 2024

29 MONDAY

30 TUESDAY

1 WEDNESDAY

Beltane
May Day
Last Quarter Moon ◑

2 THURSDAY

APRIL 2024						
S	M	T	W	T	F	S
	1	2	3	4	5	6
7	8	9	10	11	12	13
14	15	16	17	18	19	20
21	22	23	24	25	26	27
28	29	30				

3 FRIDAY

MAY 2024						
S	M	T	W	T	F	S
			1	2	3	4
5	6	7	8	9	10	11
12	13	14	15	16	17	18
19	20	21	22	23	24	25
26	27	28	29	30	31	

4 SATURDAY

5 SUNDAY

Orthodox Easter
Cinco de Mayo

MAY 2024

Sunday	Monday	Tuesday	Wednesday
29	30	31	1 Beltane May Day Last Quarter Moon
5 Orthodox Easter Cinco de Mayo	6 May Day bank holiday (UK, IRL)	7 New Moon	8
12 Mother's Day	13	14	15 First Quarter Moon
19	20 Victoria Day (CAN)	21	22
26	27 Memorial Day (US) Spring bank holiday (UK)	28	29

Thursday	Friday	Saturday
2	3	4
9	10	11
16	17	18
23	24	25
30	31	1

Full Moon ◯

Last Quarter Moon ◑

NOTES

A Beltane Happy Home Spell

Fertility, happiness, concentration, and achievements are good focuses for rituals performed during Beltane. This "kinfolk spell" can bring happiness and laughter to the home and all who reside there.

Materials

- 1 crystal (use carnelian, garnet, malachite, moss agate, or tiger's eye)
  As many pieces of paper as there are people in your family
- 1 pencil
- 3 three-foot (1 m) ribbons, in purple, white, and green
- 2 candles, in white
  A feast of spring foods

Ritual

Cleanse and empower your crystal (see pages 170–71). On each piece of paper write the following incantation:

> *"We celebrate this Beltane with food and with flame;*
> *we give you our thanks for uniting us again.*
> *Happiness and joy reign in this house,*
> *all who dwell are blessed with this spell."*

Knot the three ribbons together at the top and braid them, wrapping one over the other. Each family member must take a turn in crossing over the ribbon until all of it is braided. Tie a knot at the end. Place the braided ribbon lengthwise down the center of a table and light both candles, placing one at each end. Cook and prepare a feast including fresh spring fruits and vegetables. Lay the feast on the table. When all are seated, give each person a copy of the written incantation. Pass the empowered crystal around the table before finally placing it on top of the braided ribbon. Together, read the incantation three times. The person at the head of the table must close the ritual by saying *"So mote it be."* Proceed to enjoy your meal. After the feast, clear everything away, but leave the crystal at the center of the table for a few months. If you gather together regularly to eat your meals the magick will continue to flow.

MAY 2024

6 MONDAY

May Day bank holiday (UK, IRL)

7 TUESDAY

8 WEDNESDAY

9 THURSDAY

MAY 2024

S	M	T	W	T	F	S
			1	2	3	4
5	6	7	8	9	10	11
12	13	14	15	16	17	18
19	20	21	22	23	24	25
26	27	28	29	30	31	

10 FRIDAY

JUNE 2024

S	M	T	W	T	F	S
						1
2	3	4	5	6	7	8
9	10	11	12	13	14	15
16	17	18	19	20	21	22
23	24	25	26	27	28	29
30						

11 SATURDAY

12 SUNDAY

Mother's Day

13 MONDAY

14 TUESDAY

15 WEDNESDAY

First Quarter Moon ◗

16 THURSDAY

17 FRIDAY

18 SATURDAY

19 SUNDAY

MAY 2024

20 MONDAY

Victoria Day (CAN)

21 TUESDAY

22 WEDNESDAY

23 THURSDAY

Full Moon ○

24 FRIDAY

25 SATURDAY

26 SUNDAY

MAY 2024						
S	M	T	W	T	F	S
			1	2	3	4
5	6	7	8	9	10	11
12	13	14	15	16	17	18
19	20	21	22	23	24	25
26	27	28	29	30	31	

JUNE 2024						
S	M	T	W	T	F	S
						1
2	3	4	5	6	7	8
9	10	11	12	13	14	15
16	17	18	19	20	21	22
23	24	25	26	27	28	29
30						

27 MONDAY

Memorial Day (US)
Spring bank holiday (UK)

28 TUESDAY

29 WEDNESDAY

30 THURSDAY

Last Quarter Moon ◖

31 FRIDAY

MAY 2024						
S	M	T	W	T	F	S
			1	2	3	4
5	6	7	8	9	10	11
12	13	14	15	16	17	18
19	20	21	22	23	24	25
26	27	28	29	30	31	

1 SATURDAY

2 SUNDAY

JUNE 2024						
S	M	T	W	T	F	S
						1
2	3	4	5	6	7	8
9	10	11	12	13	14	15
16	17	18	19	20	21	22
23	24	25	26	27	28	29
30						

A Spell to Tap into Dryad Power

If you want to get as close to nature as possible, then try this spell. On a dry day, venture out into a forest or wooded area, place a blanket on the ground beneath a large tree, and sit. Oak trees are best if you can find one. As you sit, look up at the branches above you and drink in the fresh air. Place your hands on the ground and stay still for a few minutes. Say this spell quietly to yourself while concentrating on the roots beneath your fingers:

> *"From the roots on the ground to your branches of strength,*
> *I attune your power, your magickal length,*
> *Spirits of nature, wood nymph, or dryad,*
> *Entwine with my energy, make my soul glad."*

When you have said the spell a few times, stand up and place your arms around the tree, feeling the magick of the dryad coursing through your veins. Quietly repeat the spell. The longer you stay near the tree, the more power you will receive. This spell is very good if you suffer from minor ailments, as a person is thought to receive healing strength from the tree.

Sunday	Monday	Tuesday	Wednesday
26	27	28	29
2	3	4	5
9	10	11	12
16	17	18	19
Father's Day			Juneteenth (US)
23	24	25	26
30	1	2	3

Thursday	Friday	Saturday	NOTES
30	31	1	
6	7	8	
New Moon ●			
13	14	15	
	Flag Day (US) First Quarter Moon ◑		
20	21	22	
	Full Moon ○		
27	28	29	
	Last Quarter Moon ◐		
4	5	6	

JUNE 2024

3 MONDAY

4 TUESDAY

5 WEDNESDAY

6 THURSDAY

New Moon ●

7 FRIDAY

8 SATURDAY

9 SUNDAY

10 MONDAY

11 TUESDAY

12 WEDNESDAY

13 THURSDAY

14 FRIDAY

Flag Day (US)
First Quarter Moon ◐

JUNE 2024						
S	M	T	W	T	F	S
						1
2	3	4	5	6	7	8
9	10	11	12	13	14	15
16	17	18	19	20	21	22
23	24	25	26	27	28	29
30						

15 SATURDAY

16 SUNDAY

Father's Day

JULY 2024						
S	M	T	W	T	F	S
	1	2	3	4	5	6
7	8	9	10	11	12	13
14	15	16	17	18	19	20
21	22	23	24	25	26	27
28	29	30	31			

LITHA
(SUMMER SOLSTICE)
June 19–25

Midsummer brings us the longest days and shortest nights (though the dates do vary with geography and culture). Everything in the world is blooming with fruitfulness, the goddess is heavily pregnant with child, and the sun god is at his peak of virility. At this time, witches and druids celebrate the dawn and often stay up to watch the sunrise. This is a fertile time when we can rejoice in the abundance of life; however, despite this climax, we are also aware that darkness is ahead. From here on, as the sun begins to wane, the days will become shorter and the nights longer, and soon the cycle of life will be complete.

The acorn, a symbol for fertility and prosperity, is widely used as a talisman during Midsummer (as well as during Mabon, see page 32). Acorns are carried to ensure a long and rich life and sometimes are placed on windowsills during storms to ward off lightning. On Midsummer's Eve, people stay up all through the night to welcome the sunrise. Bonfires made from oak are lit on top of hills and mountains to pay respect to the sun. Once the coals cool, they are sometimes scattered atop crops to ensure a good harvest.

17 MONDAY

18 TUESDAY

19 WEDNESDAY

Juneteenth (US)

20 THURSDAY

Litha (Summer Solstice)

21 FRIDAY

Full Moon ○

22 SATURDAY

23 SUNDAY

JUNE 2024

24 MONDAY

25 TUESDAY

26 WEDNESDAY

27 THURSDAY

JUNE 2024						
S	M	T	W	T	F	S
						1
2	3	4	5	6	7	8
9	10	11	12	13	14	15
16	17	18	19	20	21	22
23	24	25	26	27	28	29
30						

28 FRIDAY

Last Quarter Moon ◐

JULY 2024						
S	M	T	W	T	F	S
	1	2	3	4	5	6
7	8	9	10	11	12	13
14	15	16	17	18	19	20
21	22	23	24	25	26	27
28	29	30	31			

29 SATURDAY

30 SUNDAY

JULY 2024

Sunday	Monday	Tuesday	Wednesday
30	1 Canada Day	2	3
7	8	9	10
14	15	16	17
21	22	23	24
Full Moon ○			
28	29	30	31 Lammas (begins at sundown)

Thursday	Friday	Saturday
4	5	6
Independence Day (US)	New Moon ●	
11	12	13
		First Quarter Moon ◐
18	19	20
25	26	27
		Last Quarter Moon ◑
1	2	3

NOTES

JULY 2024

1 MONDAY

Canada Day

2 TUESDAY

3 WEDNESDAY

4 THURSDAY

Independence Day (US)

5 FRIDAY

New Moon ⬤

6 SATURDAY

7 SUNDAY

JULY 2024

S	M	T	W	T	F	S
	1	2	3	4	5	6
7	8	9	10	11	12	13
14	15	16	17	18	19	20
21	22	23	24	25	26	27
28	29	30	31			

AUGUST 2024

S	M	T	W	T	F	S
				1	2	3
4	5	6	7	8	9	10
11	12	13	14	15	16	17
18	19	20	21	22	23	24
25	26	27	28	29	30	31

8 MONDAY

9 TUESDAY

10 WEDNESDAY

11 THURSDAY

	JULY 2024					
S	M	T	W	T	F	S
	1	2	3	4	5	6
7	8	9	10	11	12	13
14	15	16	17	18	19	20
21	22	23	24	25	26	27
28	29	30	31			

12 FRIDAY

	AUGUST 2024					
S	M	T	W	T	F	S
				1	2	3
4	5	6	7	8	9	10
11	12	13	14	15	16	17
18	19	20	21	22	23	24
25	26	27	28	29	30	31

13 SATURDAY

14 SUNDAY

First Quarter Moon ◗

4-7-8 Mindful Meditation Technique

Taking just several minutes a day to hit a spiritual pause button can help give you a new perspective, especially if you're feeling particularly emotional or stressed. For many witches, meditation is like taking a step outside of the situation where they can escape to their spiritual place, so when they're ready to come back to spellcasting, they are doing so with a refreshed mind. Here is a great exercise to try:

Gradually breathe in through the nose on the count of 4, then hold your breath for the count of 7. Slowly, breathe out through the mouth on the count of 8. Repeat this cycle, concentrating the entire time on your breathing. Notice that when you inhale your breath is cooler, and as you exhale it gets warmer. Your mind might start to meander, and you might start thinking of everyday issues or problems. If this happens, envision those intruding thoughts being set aside, to be addressed at another time.

After a while, you may start to feel floaty; this is a prelude to astral projection and is nothing to worry about. What do you feel? Can you hear voices in your head? What might they be telling you? Some people report that they hear ethereal music or bells ringing in the distance. Concentrate on the sounds and listen. Often, visions will appear behind closed eyes, which you might later want to record in your journal. Some people have even described seeing snippets of their past lives during this type of meditation.

15 MONDAY

16 TUESDAY

17 WEDNESDAY

18 THURSDAY

19 FRIDAY

20 SATURDAY

21 SUNDAY

Full Moon ◯

JULY 2024

22 MONDAY

23 TUESDAY

24 WEDNESDAY

25 THURSDAY

JULY 2024						
S	M	T	W	T	F	S
	1	2	3	4	5	6
7	8	9	10	11	12	13
14	15	16	17	18	19	20
21	22	23	24	25	26	27
28	29	30	31			

26 FRIDAY

AUGUST 2024						
S	M	T	W	T	F	S
				1	2	3
4	5	6	7	8	9	10
11	12	13	14	15	16	17
18	19	20	21	22	23	24
25	26	27	28	29	30	31

27 SATURDAY

28 SUNDAY

Last Quarter Moon ◗

29 MONDAY

30 TUESDAY

31 WEDNESDAY

Lammas (begins at sundown)

1 THURSDAY

JULY 2024						
S	M	T	W	T	F	S
	1	2	3	4	5	6
7	8	9	10	11	12	13
14	15	16	17	18	19	20
21	22	23	24	25	26	27
28	29	30	31			

2 FRIDAY

3 SATURDAY

4 SUNDAY

New Moon

AUGUST 2024						
S	M	T	W	T	F	S
				1	2	3
4	5	6	7	8	9	10
11	12	13	14	15	16	17
18	19	20	21	22	23	24
25	26	27	28	29	30	31

LAMMAS

July 31 (sunset)—August 1

Lammas or Lughnasadh is a Pagan Thanksgiving celebration that traditionally commemorated the year's first grain harvest. The garden is all-important to modern witches, so Wiccan growers often take this opportunity to stockpile their food, blanching homegrown vegetables to freeze and eat at a later date. Witches often freeze or dry their herbs for use in spells and recipes during the colder months. The making of jam and chutney is also traditional at Lammas, so roll up your sleeves and get to work in the kitchen.

Little poppets and ornamental charms made from corn are placed on the altar in thanks to Mother Earth for her many offerings. They are a symbol of good luck and fertility. You can make your own or purchase them online. Sunflowers are by far the most general to use in spellcraft at this time of year because their heads are heavy with seed. Witches sometimes make sunflower crowns to wear during rituals.

Exercising your creativity and self-reflecting on all you have accomplished this year are also important parts of Lammas.

AUGUST 2024

Sunday	Monday	Tuesday	Wednesday
28	29	30	31
4 New Moon ●	5	6	7
11	12 First Quarter Moon ◐	13	14
18	19 Full Moon ○	20	21
25	26 Summer Bank Holiday (UK) Last Quarter Moon ◑	27	28

Thursday	Friday	Saturday	NOTES
1	2	3	
8	9	10	
15	16	17	
22	23	24	
29	30	31	

AUGUST 2024

5 MONDAY

6 TUESDAY

7 WEDNESDAY

8 THURSDAY

AUGUST 2024						
S	M	T	W	T	F	S
				1	2	3
4	5	6	7	8	9	10
11	12	13	14	15	16	17
18	19	20	21	22	23	24
25	26	27	28	29	30	31

9 FRIDAY

SEPTEMBER 2024						
S	M	T	W	T	F	S
1	2	3	4	5	6	7
8	9	10	11	12	13	14
15	16	17	18	19	20	21
22	23	24	25	26	27	28
29	30					

10 SATURDAY

11 SUNDAY

12 MONDAY

First Quarter Moon ◐

13 TUESDAY

14 WEDNESDAY

15 THURSDAY

16 FRIDAY

17 SATURDAY

18 SUNDAY

AUGUST 2024

19 MONDAY

Full Moon ○

20 TUESDAY

21 WEDNESDAY

22 THURSDAY

AUGUST 2024

S	M	T	W	T	F	S
				1	2	3
4	5	6	7	8	9	10
11	12	13	14	15	16	17
18	19	20	21	22	23	24
25	26	27	28	29	30	31

23 FRIDAY

SEPTEMBER 2024

S	M	T	W	T	F	S
1	2	3	4	5	6	7
8	9	10	11	12	13	14
15	16	17	18	19	20	21
22	23	24	25	26	27	28
29	30					

24 SATURDAY

25 SUNDAY

Casting Spells to Music

Researchers are studying how certain sounds, such as music, beneficially stimulate the vagus nerve, our longest and most complex cranial nerve. It extends from the brain stem down to the intestines, branching out to the heart, lungs, abdomen, and more. Positively stimulating the vagus nerve can reduce stress, benefiting your entire nervous system. Music has been shown to help alleviate depression and pain in post-surgical patients. When you incorporate soothing sounds into your rituals, you're launching your intentions into the ether from a solid and steady base.

You don't have to stream orchestral music to get the benefits. When witchcraft was first practiced, it was usually outside. Witches played whatever instruments they had on hand, usually a drum or sticks that they beat in a rhythmic pattern. Chants were sung to call upon spirits for assistance, or to focus and clarify intentions. They called on other witches to join their circle for community and support.

To carry that same energy over into today's modern spellcasting, get creative! If you already know how to play an instrument, think about how to incorporate it into your rituals. For example, the flute is a portable instrument that you can take anywhere—but what if you play the piano? You could bring a smaller portable keyboard when spellcasting in the woods, or you might want to do cast your spell indoors—sitting down at the piano to play during a ritual. Or you might record yourself and play the recording wherever you happen to be. Alternatively, you could play to relax your mind and spirit before casting a spell.

AUGUST/SEPTEMBER 2024

26 MONDAY

Summer Bank Holiday (UK)
Last Quarter Moon

27 TUESDAY

28 WEDNESDAY

29 THURSDAY

AUGUST 2024						
S	M	T	W	T	F	S
				1	2	3
4	5	6	7	8	9	10
11	12	13	14	15	16	17
18	19	20	21	22	23	24
25	26	27	28	29	30	31

30 FRIDAY

SEPTEMBER 2024						
S	M	T	W	T	F	S
1	2	3	4	5	6	7
8	9	10	11	12	13	14
15	16	17	18	19	20	21
22	23	24	25	26	27	28
29	30					

31 SATURDAY

1 SUNDAY

SEPTEMBER 2024

Sunday	Monday	Tuesday	Wednesday
1	2 Labor Day (US/CAN) New Moon ●	3	4
8	9	10	11 First Quarter Moon ◑
15	16	17 Full Moon ○	18
22 Mabon	23	24 Last Quarter Moon ◐	25
29	30	31	1

Thursday	Friday	Saturday	NOTES
5	6	7	
12	13	14	
19	20	21	
26	27	28	
2	3	4	

2 MONDAY

Labor Day (US/CAN)
New Moon ●

---

3 TUESDAY

---

4 WEDNESDAY

---

5 THURSDAY

---

6 FRIDAY

---

7 SATURDAY | **8** SUNDAY

SEPTEMBER 2024

9 MONDAY

10 TUESDAY

11 WEDNESDAY

First Quarter Moon ◑

12 THURSDAY

13 FRIDAY

14 SATURDAY

15 SUNDAY

A Mabon Spell

Mabon is a great time for prosperity and money rituals—and for spells concerning security, safety, protection, confidence, and financial security—so perform a general money spell, like the one given here, on Mabon.

Materials

- 2 small pieces of sunstone
- 1 apple, any kind
  Paring knife
- 2 tealight candles, in red, green, orange, or yellow
  Items that represent Mabon (see pages 8–9)

Ritual

Cleanse and empower your crystals (see pages 170–71). Hold one sunstone in each hand while imagining that an upturned, gold cornucopia is spilling gold coins all over you. Silently ask the universe to bless you with a better financial situation and envisage yourself paying off all your bills with ease. Place the crystals on the altar and cut the apple in half, widthwise, with the knife. Note that the seeded area in each half forms a pentacle star. Slice the bottom of each apple half so it sits flat. Carefully cut in a circle around the stars, carving out a hole in each apple half large enough to place a tealight candle inside. Place the apples side by side on your altar and insert a tealight candle inside each hold before lighting them. Finally, place the crystals in front of each apple half. Decorate your altar with Mabon items, and then recite the following spell seven times:

> *"I call upon the god and goddess to bring stability to my life and grace me with a purse of wealth, I show gratitude and thankfulness for your blessings already bestowed. Turn around my fortune and let me sleep easy, knowing that my financial life is settled and in balance."*

After you've recited the spell seven times, close the ritual by adding **"So mote it be."** Then allow the candles to burn down (supervised) until they extinguish themselves. Take the apple halves and place them as an offering under a tree. Keep the crystals somewhere at home. In the coming weeks, your finances may start to improve.

SEPTEMBER 2024

16 MONDAY

17 TUESDAY

Full Moon ○

18 WEDNESDAY

19 THURSDAY

SEPTEMBER 2024

S	M	T	W	T	F	S
1	2	3	4	5	6	7
8	9	10	11	12	13	14
15	16	17	18	19	20	21
22	23	24	25	26	27	28
29	30					

20 FRIDAY

OCTOBER 2024

S	M	T	W	T	F	S
		1	2	3	4	5
6	7	8	9	10	11	12
13	14	15	16	17	18	19
20	21	22	23	24	25	26
27	28	29	30	31		

21 SATURDAY

22 SUNDAY

Mabon (Autumnal Equinox)

23 MONDAY

24 TUESDAY

Last Quarter Moon ◑

25 WEDNESDAY

26 THURSDAY

SEPTEMBER 2024						
S	M	T	W	T	F	S
1	2	3	4	5	6	7
8	9	10	11	12	13	14
15	16	17	18	19	20	21
22	23	24	25	26	27	28
29	30					

27 FRIDAY

28 SATURDAY

29 SUNDAY

OCTOBER 2024						
S	M	T	W	T	F	S
		1	2	3	4	5
6	7	8	9	10	11	12
13	14	15	16	17	18	19
20	21	22	23	24	25	26
27	28	29	30	31		

DRYAS

OCTOBER 2024

Sunday	Monday	Tuesday	Wednesday
30	31	1	2 Rosh Hashanah (begins at sundown) New Moon ●
6	7	8	9
13	14 Indigenous People's Day Columbus Day (US) Thanksgiving (CAN)	15	16
20	21	22	23
27	28	29	30

Thursday	Friday	Saturday	NOTES
3	4	5	
10 First Quarter Moon ◐	11 Yom Kippur (begins at sundown)	12	
17 Full Moon ○	18	19	
24 Last Quarter Moon ◑	25	26	
31 Samhain Halloween	1	2	

Oil to Banish Negativity

Sometimes, negative energy clings to us, especially if we have been going through a rough time or if we've been feeling unhappy. Once negative energy takes hold it can be difficult to rid yourself of it. This spell is a great negativity cleanser and will spiritually disinfect you and any area you anoint with the oil.

Materials

- 2 fresh chive stems, chopped into tiny pieces
- 1 dried sage leaf, crumbled or chopped
- Glass jar
- 2 teaspoons (10 ml) extra-virgin olive oil
- 5 drops frankincense essential oil
- 1 white tealight candle
- Tea strainer
- Mini funnel
- 10 ml glass bottle with screw-top lid

Ritual

On a new moon phase, place the chopped chives and sage leaves in the glass jar and pour the olive oil on top. Sprinkle with the frankincense oil and mix well. Light the candle and recite the following spell:

> *"I charge this oil with all things positive.*
> *All negative vibes shall be gone."*

Let the candle burn down (attended). Let the mixture steep for three days. Strain the oil through the tea strainer and use the funnel to transfer it into the 10 ml glass bottle. Screw the lid on. Take the contents of the tea strainer and scattered them outside your front door to give you added protection from anything untoward. Use the oil to anoint candles or crystals, or drizzle it over potpourri. Smear it on house door jambs or your car dashboard to keep negativity away.

SEPTEMBER/OCTOBER 2024

30 MONDAY

1 TUESDAY

2 WEDNESDAY

Rosh Hashanah (begins at sundown)
New Moon ⬤

3 THURSDAY

OCTOBER 2024						
S	M	T	W	T	F	S
		1	2	3	4	5
6	7	8	9	10	11	12
13	14	15	16	17	18	19
20	21	22	23	24	25	26
27	28	29	30	31		

4 FRIDAY

NOVEMBER 2024						
S	M	T	W	T	F	S
					1	2
3	4	5	6	7	8	9
10	11	12	13	14	15	16
17	18	19	20	21	22	23
24	25	26	27	28	29	30

5 SATURDAY

6 SUNDAY

7 MONDAY

8 TUESDAY

9 WEDNESDAY

10 THURSDAY

First Quarter Moon ◐

11 FRIDAY

Yom Kippur (begins at sundown)

12 SATURDAY

13 SUNDAY

OCTOBER 2024						
S	M	T	W	T	F	S
		1	2	3	4	5
6	7	8	9	10	11	12
13	14	15	16	17	18	19
20	21	22	23	24	25	26
27	28	29	30	31		

NOVEMBER 2024						
S	M	T	W	T	F	S
					1	2
3	4	5	6	7	8	9
10	11	12	13	14	15	16
17	18	19	20	21	22	23
24	25	26	27	28	29	30

14 MONDAY

Indigenous People's Day
Columbus Day (US)
Thanksgiving (CAN)

15 TUESDAY

16 WEDNESDAY

17 THURSDAY

Full Moon ○

18 FRIDAY

19 SATURDAY

20 SUNDAY

OCTOBER 2024

21 MONDAY

22 TUESDAY

23 WEDNESDAY

24 THURSDAY

Last Quarter Moon ◗

25 FRIDAY

26 SATURDAY

27 SUNDAY

28 MONDAY

---

29 TUESDAY

---

30 WEDNESDAY

---

31 THURSDAY

Samhain, Halloween

OCTOBER 2024						
S	M	T	W	T	F	S
		1	2	3	4	5
6	7	8	9	10	11	12
13	14	15	16	17	18	19
20	21	22	23	24	25	26
27	28	29	30	31		

1 FRIDAY

New Moon ●

NOVEMBER 2024						
S	M	T	W	T	F	S
					1	2
3	4	5	6	7	8	9
10	11	12	13	14	15	16
17	18	19	20	21	22	23
24	25	26	27	28	29	30

2 SATURDAY

3 SUNDAY

Daylight Saving Time Ends
(US, CAN)

A Samhain Spell

A nice traditional exercise to do at Samhain is to reach out and communicate with any deceased loved ones. Perform this ritual during the evening of October 31.

Materials

- 1 piece of spirit quart
- 1 sprig of fresh rosemary
- Small dish
- 1 teaspoon of dried vervain
- ½ teaspoon of white pepper
- 1 bay leaf
- Photograph of your deceased loved one(s)
- 1 candle, in purple

Ritual

Cleanse your crystal (see pages 170–71). To empower it, cup it in your hands and think about your loved one and gather your memories of time you spent together. After doing this for a few minutes, place the crystal on the altar, then tear the leaves off the rosemary sprig and place them in the dish. Add the dried vervain, white pepper, and bay leaf. Rest the photograph of your deceased loved one on the altar and place the crystal on top. Light the purple candle and say the following incantation thirteen times:

> *"I raise the veil and call out to you; see my face, hear my voice,*
> *This Samhain I summon you and speak with you; this is my choice,*
> *I raise the veil and reach to you; feel my touch, sense my power."*

After you've recited the spell thirteen times, close the ritual by adding **"So mote it be."** While the candle is burning, talk aloud to your loved one. Say anything you want; this is your time to express your feelings and be at one with them. It's not uncommon for you to sense that you're not alone. When the candle has burned for about an hour (attended), extinguish it; then take the bowl of herbs and the crystal and place them next to your bed. If your loved one has heard your message, they may visit you in your dreams.

NOVEMBER 2024

Sunday	Monday	Tuesday	Wednesday
27	28	29	30
3 Daylight Saving Time Ends (US, CAN)	4	5 Election Day (US)	6
10	11 Veterans Day	12	13
17	18	19	20
24	25	26	27

Thursday	Friday	Saturday	NOTES
31	1 New Moon ●	2	
7	8	9 First Quarter Moon ◑	
14	15 Full Moon ○	16	
21	22 Last Quarter Moon ◐	23	
28 Thanksgiving (US)	29	30	

Snow Moon Ritual

November is a particularly good time to use the moon to bring about peacefulness. During this time, the Snow Moon promotes tranquility and contemplation.

If it's possible, go outside and bathe yourself in the light (or dark) of the moon's energy to perform any sleep or calming rituals before you go to bed. This is relatively easy if you live in a temperate climate, but it will be more challenging if it is a freezing evening. (Most people don't find it comfortable or relaxing to be outside at night in the dead of winter!) If this is the case, you can still go ahead and perform your ritual near a window—you're still accessing the moon's healing rays, and you are keeping yourself warm and cozy, which will help to promote a good night's rest.

NOVEMBER 2024

4 MONDAY

5 TUESDAY

Election Day (US)

6 WEDNESDAY

7 THURSDAY

NOVEMBER 2024						
S	M	T	W	T	F	S
					1	2
3	4	5	6	7	8	9
10	11	12	13	14	15	16
17	18	19	20	21	22	23
24	25	26	27	28	29	30

8 FRIDAY

DECEMBER 2024						
S	M	T	W	T	F	S
1	2	3	4	5	6	7
8	9	10	11	12	13	14
15	16	17	18	19	20	21
22	23	24	25	26	27	28
29	30	31				

9 SATURDAY

First Quarter Moon ◑

10 SUNDAY

11 MONDAY

Veterans Day

12 TUESDAY

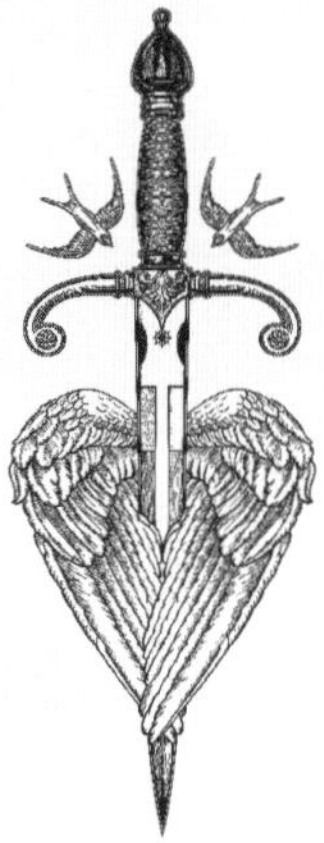

13 WEDNESDAY

14 THURSDAY

15 FRIDAY

Full Moon ○

16 SATURDAY

17 SUNDAY

NOVEMBER 2024

18 MONDAY

19 TUESDAY

20 WEDNESDAY

21 THURSDAY

22 FRIDAY

Last Quarter Moon ◑

23 SATURDAY

24 SUNDAY

NOVEMBER/DECEMBER 2024

25 MONDAY

26 TUESDAY

27 WEDNESDAY

28 THURSDAY

Thanksgiving (US)

<table>
<tr><td colspan="7" align="center">NOVEMBER 2024</td></tr>
<tr><td>S</td><td>M</td><td>T</td><td>W</td><td>T</td><td>F</td><td>S</td></tr>
<tr><td></td><td></td><td></td><td></td><td></td><td>1</td><td>2</td></tr>
<tr><td>3</td><td>4</td><td>5</td><td>6</td><td>7</td><td>8</td><td>9</td></tr>
<tr><td>10</td><td>11</td><td>12</td><td>13</td><td>14</td><td>15</td><td>16</td></tr>
<tr><td>17</td><td>18</td><td>19</td><td>20</td><td>21</td><td>22</td><td>23</td></tr>
<tr><td>24</td><td>25</td><td>26</td><td>27</td><td>28</td><td>29</td><td>30</td></tr>
</table>

29 FRIDAY

<table>
<tr><td colspan="7" align="center">DECEMBER 2024</td></tr>
<tr><td>S</td><td>M</td><td>T</td><td>W</td><td>T</td><td>F</td><td>S</td></tr>
<tr><td>1</td><td>2</td><td>3</td><td>4</td><td>5</td><td>6</td><td>7</td></tr>
<tr><td>8</td><td>9</td><td>10</td><td>11</td><td>12</td><td>13</td><td>14</td></tr>
<tr><td>15</td><td>16</td><td>17</td><td>18</td><td>19</td><td>20</td><td>21</td></tr>
<tr><td>22</td><td>23</td><td>24</td><td>25</td><td>26</td><td>27</td><td>28</td></tr>
<tr><td>29</td><td>30</td><td>31</td><td></td><td></td><td></td><td></td></tr>
</table>

30 SATURDAY

1 SUNDAY

New Moon ●

DECEMBER 2024

Sunday	Monday	Tuesday	Wednesday
1 New Moon ●	2	3	4
8 First Quarter Moon ◑	9	10	11
15 Full Moon ○	16	17	18
22 Last Quarter Moon ◐	23	24	25 Christmas Day Hanukkah (begins at sundown)
29	30 New Moon ●	31 New Year's Eve	1

Thursday	Friday	Saturday	NOTES
5	6	7	
12	13	14	
19	20	21 Yule (Winter Solstice)	
26 Kwanzaa Boxing Day (CAN, UK)	27	28	
2	3	4	

2 MONDAY

3 TUESDAY

4 WEDNESDAY

5 THURSDAY

6 FRIDAY

7 SATURDAY

8 SUNDAY

First Quarter Moon ◗

DECEMBER 2024

9 MONDAY

10 TUESDAY

11 WEDNESDAY

12 THURSDAY

DECEMBER 2024

S	M	T	W	T	F	S
1	2	3	4	5	6	7
8	9	10	11	12	13	14
15	16	17	18	19	20	21
22	23	24	25	26	27	28
29	30	31				

13 FRIDAY

JANUARY 2025

S	M	T	W	T	F	S
			1	2	3	4
5	6	7	8	9	10	11
12	13	14	15	16	17	18
19	20	21	22	23	24	25
26	27	28	29	30	31	

14 SATURDAY

15 SUNDAY

Full Moon ◯

A Yuletide Spell

Spellwork during Yuletide should be performed with happiness and harmony in mind. Any intentions related to love, romance, and gratitude are sure to be successful. Witches love to cast spells at this time of year, showing thanks for the past twelve months and ensuring a safe and abundant winter in the months ahead.

Materials

1 piece of crystal (see list on page 6)	2–4 candles, in red, green, or gold
Items that represent Yule (see list on page 6)	Wand (optional)
	Small bell
Celtic Christmas-themed music	

Ritual

Cleanse and empower your crystal (see pages 170–71). On December 21, set up your altar with items that represent Yule along with the candles in the color(s) of your choice. Light the candles. Place the crystal on your altar, next to the candles. Play Celtic Christmas music to set the scene for a balanced and settled ritual. If you have a wand, rotate it clockwise over your altar to cast a circle (alternatively, you can use your pointer finger). Next, ring the bell for a minute or two to clear away unwanted energies left behind from the previous year and magickally sterilize your workspace. Kneel or sit in front of the altar and speak the following incantation twelve times:

> *"Yule is upon us. I thank the gods for all the blessings bestowed upon me.*
> *Keep me safe and free from harm as wintertime appears. Blessed be."*

After you've recited the spell twelve times, close it by adding ***"So mote it be."*** You can also create your own spell by writing yourself an ode to Yule.

DECEMBER 2024

16 MONDAY

17 TUESDAY

18 WEDNESDAY

19 THURSDAY

20 FRIDAY

21 SATURDAY

22 SUNDAY

Yule (Winter Solstice)

Last Quarter Moon ◑

23 MONDAY

24 TUESDAY

25 WEDNESDAY

Christmas Day
Hanukkah (begins at sundown)

26 THURSDAY

Kwanzaa
Boxing Day (CAN, UK)

27 FRIDAY

28 SATURDAY

29 SUNDAY

DEC 2024/JAN 2025

30 MONDAY

New Moon ●

31 TUESDAY

New Year's Eve

1 WEDNESDAY

New Year's Day

2 THURSDAY

3 FRIDAY

4 SATURDAY

5 SUNDAY

APPENDIXES

COLOR MAGICK

Witches rely heavily on color magick. Different colors can signify different intentions or themes, so certain candles and items should be specifically colored when used in spells. Before reaching into your candle drawer or laying out your altar cloth, consider which color will work best to promote your specific intention.

BLACK is often avoided in spellcasting because it is commonly used in dark magick. However, more experienced witches can use black to banish anything or anyone negative. If used correctly, it can be beneficial.

BLUE stands for truth, wisdom, stable emotions, meditation, psychic insight, protection, and patience.

BROWN can help you tune into the natural world. It assists with concentration and decision-making and can be used in matters related to friendship, including relationships with animals.

GOLD is the color used for monetary matters, triumph in competition, improving intelligence, promoting health, and rejuvenation of the mind, body, and spirit.

GREEN bolsters spells for money, prosperity, success, and luck. It is helpful with career matters and with fertility.

ORANGE helps with business matters (including selling property), memory, and stamina. If you need to find lost property, decrease your fears, favorably settle legal issues, or succeed in a new job, then incorporate some orange into your altar.

PINK works well for compassion and spiritual healing, and in mending broken relationships. You can also rely on pink to improve existing relationships or to attract love.

PURPLE promotes peace, healing, spiritual protection, and psychic visions. It can be helpful for those wishing to practice astral projection. For everyday, practical rituals, use purple to boost business, help in the search for a new job, and influence anything to do with investments.

RED helps with intentions focused on courage, passion, and strength. The energy of red can increase one's attractiveness and sexual energy, and arouses passion. It will help keep enemies at bay.

SILVER boosts psychic abilities (including intuition), decreases the negative energy of the mind or environment, clarifies dream visions, and helps one connect with the Mother Goddess.

WHITE calls on angels and spirit guides, invokes those who have passed, encourages harmony in relationships or environments, and purifies a home. White can also be viewed as the blank canvas of colors; it can be used in any ritual. You can replace any candle color with white if you don't know what color is the best for a specific spell or if you don't have a particular color candle on hand.

YELLOW helps with creativity, learning, and concentration. It increases energy and provides protection while one is traveling. This color also helps with matters concerning the head, including headaches and mood swings.

CLEANSING AND EMPOWERING CRYSTALS

While crystals can attract positive energy, they can also hold on to negative energy, so crystals that are used in clearing negative energy should be cleansed and re-empowered before being used again. You might notice that after such a ritual, your crystal will feel hot or heavy, or look lackluster. If you have a crystal you've been relying on for some time and it seems to have lost its oomph, you should think about giving it a boost.

Cleansing Your Crystal

There are multiple ways to cleanse and recharge your crystals, so here are a few to get you started:

SMUDGE WITH SAGE: In a safe area or outside, waft the crystal through the smoke for about thirty seconds.

FRESHWATER BATH: Submerge your stones in fresh water from a stream, spring, pond, or lake. Note: There are some crystals that should not be exposed to water though. Selenite can dissolve, and hematite will rust when left in water too long.

SALTWATER BATH: Fill a glass or ceramic bowl with salt water and soak your crystal for up to an hour or longer as needed. Dispose of the saltwater and rinse the crystal in cool spring water. Note: Avoid using salt with porous stones like opal, and pyrite and lapis; see above note on selenite and hematite.

SUNLIGHT AND MOONLIGHT: Place your stones outside during the day for a few hours when the sun is at its height or overnight under the moonlight; a full moon phase is best. Lay them on the ground, on an outside table, or on a windowsill. Make sure that light-sensitive crystals such as citrine and amethyst are not left in the heat of the sun for more than thirty minutes.

SEA SALT: Pour pure sea salt into a large-enough bowl, completely covering the crystals. Let them sit for a few hours, and then dispose of the salt. See above note in Saltwater Bath.

TIBETAN BELLS: The sound from the chime of Tibetan bells retunes crystals and gives them a healing boost.

Empowering Your Crystal

After you have cleansed your chosen crystal by using one of the methods listed opposite and above, the next step is to empower it.

When you do this, you are making a personal connection with it so that it recognizes your energy and will work its magick alongside you. The following procedure must be performed every single time you conduct a crystal spell.

1. **Prepare a quiet room in the house.** Light some candles and dot them around the area where you will be sitting.
2. **Play some beautiful music.** Stream some soothing meditating or New Age–style music.
3. **Sit quietly in a chair and cup the crystal in both hands.** Close your eyes and think about the spell you want to perform. Imagine the clear-cut outcome of the spell, and visualize positive energy flowing from you into the stone. Continue with this visualization for at least two minutes.
4. **Speaking out loud, ask the crystal to project its magick.** A short affirmation could go something like this: *"With the magick inside of me, I invite you to release your power to me. Deliver your mighty energy and help me this day."*
5. **Tell the crystal precisely what you want it to do.**
6. **Place your crystal on a table or worktop and create a ring of salt around it.** Circle the salt with seven white tealight candles; light them. This protective circle will shine an invisible light of power directly upward. Stand over the crystal so that your face is directly above the stone. (If you have long hair, please tie it back and be cautious of the flames.) Repeat these words seven times:

"I empower this crystal with magickal light.
I inhale the light this night."

Once you have said the mantra seven times, close by saying, *"So mote it be."*

CRYSTAL TOOLKIT

Here we list the twenty most commonly used crystals—tried-and-true essentials that belong in every witch's collection and should be enough to get you started on the path of crystal witchery. As you experiment with each of these crystals (and others), you may find it valuable to make notes of which stones can be used for what spells in your personal Book of Shadows, and which had the best results.

AGATE

This banded, semiprecious gemstone is a form of microcrystalline quartz. To help settle painful emotions, lie down and place it over the heart. Agate radiates power and calms tempers. It is also a powerful healing stone, cleanses the aura, improves concentration, helps one to find the truth, and promotes self-confidence.

Color(s): Common colors include blue, brown, gray, moss, onyx, and pink.

FIRE AGATE

This variety of agate brings safety and protection to its owner, giving support and courage during difficult times. It repels negativity, protects from the evil eye or ill-wishers, and acts as a force field, preventing negative thoughts from reaching its owner. Carry fire agate with you if you have an enemy or know that someone is thinking ill of you.

Color(s): Deep reddish brown with accents of orange, red, green, and gold.

AMBER

Amber actually isn't a crystal; it is fossilized tree resin that has long been valued for its color and beauty. Amber is used widely for healing. If worn continuously around the throat or wrist, it can balance the chakras and ward off sadness. If you are feeling deflated or hopeless, wear an amber necklace, bracelet, or ring. Amber also brings about stability and enhances wisdom.

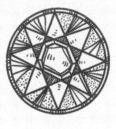

Color(s): Golden brown to lemon yellow to milky white; more rarely red, green, and even blue.

AMETHYST

Easily recognizable for its violet hue, this variety of quartz is one of the most potent crystals used by spellcasters. Amethyst combats insomnia and protects against nightmares. It has a beautiful calming effect and can help with meditation or when one would like to tune into a more spiritual vibration. Fretful babies and children react exceptionally well to this stone if it is placed in their bedroom (high up and out of reach for safety, of course).

Color(s): Purple

ANGELITE

A variety of anhydrite from Peru, this pale blue mineral can assist in powerful healing. As its name suggests, angelite is used primarily for contact and communication with the higher realm. This stone increases telepathic communication, enables astral projection, helps reveal inner truths, and can magickally transform a person's compassion and empathy. Summon an angel every time you cast a spell by placing angelite on your altar.

Color(s): Usually blue flecked with soft white spots, but can also be colorless or violet

AQUAMARINE

A powerful force against all things negative, this semiprecious crystal is a member of the beryl family (see page 174). It promotes intelligence and clairvoyant abilities and soothes during meditation and healing. Aquamarine also clears the mind, calms the soul, and is especially good at helping one combat fear. It's also quite effective when entering a nerve-racking situation. Carry aquamarine if you plan to travel over water.

Color(s): Greenish blue; the purest translucent varieties can appear sky blue

BERYL

Beryl encapsulates a large variety of semiprecious crystals, including aquamarine and emerald. No matter the variety, beryl deescalates stressful situations and clears away negative energies. A beryl is also an excellent choice for scrying and is often used to create crystal balls. Hold a beryl stone in your hand while performing divination magick, or fix a small piece into your wand.

Color(s)/Varieties: Varied across many varieties, including aquamarine, bixbite, emerald, goshenite, heliodor, maxixe, and morganite, among others.

BLOODSTONE

Also known as heliotrope, this magickal crystal is a variety of jasper with immense power. Weather witches tend to lean toward using this stone, as it was once believed to control weather. Placing this crystal in a small bowl of water by one's bedside will bring restful sleep and sweet dreams. Bloodstone is also a stone of creativity, so it is suitable for any rituals that involve boosting the imagination. It can also help with removing ghosts or spirits and repelling danger.

Color(s): Dark red, green, or brown, or a combination of the three, typically with red inclusions of hematite

CARNELIAN

Carnelian is a semiprecious stone in the chalcedony family. It possesses magickal properties that cleanse and restore other crystals. If placed among other crystals or inside a geode, it permeates powerful energies and rids other crystals of contamination. Carnelian provides one with inner strength and courage in difficult situations. It helps with mental preparation for childbirth; is thought to influence wealth and abundance; calms angry emotions; and stems lethargy.

Color(s): Red, orange, brownish-red

CELESTITE

Also called celestine, this mineral derives its name from the Latin *caelestis*, meaning "celestial" or "heavenly." Naturally, celestite helps its user reach a higher power and connect with the angels and divine guides. Many crystal witches tend to have a piece of this gemstone somewhere nearby when spellcasting. Celestite can help heal unhealthy relationships, enhance scrying abilities, soothe anxiety, and sharpen the mind.

Color(s): Pale blue, pale pink, pale brown, white, yellow, or colorless

CITRINE

This cheery, bright yellow variety of quartz carries the power of the sun and removes blocks and obstacles from life. Trying to sell your home? Bury citrine chips in the garden to help speed up the sale. Citrine also promotes good fortune and success, healing and chakra balancing, wealth, and prosperity; helps heal warring families; enhances concentration; and aids with menstrual problems and menopause.

Color(s): Ranges in color from pale to golden yellow, honey-toned shades, or nearly brown

FLUORITE

Fluorite is the original fluorescent mineral; it is the inspiration for the term *fluorescence* due to its behavior under ultraviolet light. (Let your fluorite sit in bright sunshine for a few minutes, then take it into a dark room. It might glow!) It is a useful stone for protection, drawing out any negativity around a person. It also works as a learning aid, so it is excellent to use in spells that boost mental concentration. Fluorite can help change fixed behavior; calm emotions, encourage reorganization, and promote happiness in relationships.

Color(s): Translucent purple, yellow, brown, green and blue; some specimens glow blue-violet under a black light.

MOLDAVITE

This form of tektite is believed to have been formed by a meteorite impact in Europe that took place around 15 million years ago. This stone is intensely powerful and, if the science is accurate, is of extraterrestrial origin. It is so effective that many people describe a feeling of nausea when holding it. Moldavite enhances psychic abilities and divination and helps heal emotional turmoil. Because it is fragile, never cleanse moldavite with salt; it will scratch the surface.

Color(s): Forest green, olive green, or bluish green

MOONSTONE

Identifiable for its lustrous, opalescent appearance, moonstone is a semiprecious stone associated with the moon and its phases. This crystal is perfect for the cycles and changes that life brings. Worn frequently by psychics, moonstone magnifies intuition and expands the mind. Moonstone aids in emotional healing, menstrual health, and general wellness in women; it also helps men relate to their feminine side.

Color(s): Pearly white, cream, blue, yellow, green, or translucent

ONYX

A variety of chalcedony and a cousin of agate, deep-black onyx brings strength to both the person who needs it and to the spell at hand. Onyx gives strength, vigor, and courage; dispels lustful urges; and is useful in summoning guidance. It also lends itself well to past-life issues that may be affecting present-day circumstances.

Color(s): Black, dark gray, sometimes banded

QUARTZ

With dozens of varieties and virtually endless uses, quartz is the second-most abundant mineral in Earth's continental crust (after feldspar). It is probably one of the more powerful stones that can be used for magickally unblocking situations. It is an essential healing stone, aligning the chakras and casting out negativity. It also boosts memory and concentration and unlocks memories, heals emotional issues, and is believed to invigorate overall health.

Color(s)/Varieties: Nearly every color, including colorless; major varieties include agate, amethyst, carnelian, citrine, jasper, rock crystal, rose, smoky, and tiger's eye, among others.

ROSE QUARTZ

This popular, pink-hued gemstone is a perfect tool for any type of love, be it eros (romantic), *agape* (universal), *storge* (family), *philia* (friendship), or *philautia* (self). It attracts love, heals relationships, brings about harmonious marriages and unions, and helps one to express and release emotions Rose quartz is the most frequently used crystal for any ritual pertaining to affairs of the heart.

Color(s): Hues of pink

TIGER'S EYE

This banded brown gemstone has amazing protective qualities and will repel anyone wishing ill upon you. It is sometimes used by witches to achieve kundalini awakening, or the stirring of the divine energy that lies at the base of the spine. Tiger's eye also improves meditation, removes curses, provides protection from anything negative, and allows a person to overcome self-doubt.

Color(s): Brown, red, and yellow; often banded

TOURMALINE

This stone attunes itself with anything magical and can eliminate any negativity. Witches like to protect themselves when casting spells and so this stone can be placed on the altar during any ritual. Black tourmaline is especially protective. Tourmaline can also help heal sadness, aid in business matters, and promote happiness.

Color(s): Black, brown, gold, green and pink

TURQUOISE

Turquoise, easily recognized for its bright bluish green color, is a mineral commonly used for protection against danger. It also helps to improves intuition, release inhibitions, and stabilize mood.

Color(s): Light blue, bluish green, and deep green or blue, some with darker veins or matrices

CANDLES IN RITUAL

Candles have always played a major part in spell-casting rituals, and although it is perfectly acceptable to simply voice our needs and desires, sometimes spells carry much more potency when we focus on the issues with a flame or two. Fire is a powerful element, so when a spell is recited over a lit candle, the message is transported to the universe much more forcefully and the desire directed back to us in due course. In Wiccan circles, this is called a candle ritual or candle magick. Most Wiccans have a collection of candles in assorted colors for every occasion. Each candle color has its own significance and therefore tends to work better for a particular problem (see pages 168–69 for more on colors in magick).

The size of the candle you use is not important, but most rituals suggest that you allow the candle to burn all the way down, so it's best to use either a short taper or a tea light to reduce burning time. To inscribe a tea light, use a fine pin and keep the wording short.

Preparing Your Candle

Before you cast any spell with a candle, it is important to prepare the candle first. To begin, cleanse it by wiping it with a clean damp cloth. This will ensure that any unwanted energy is washed away. Take a sharp knife or pin and inscribe your desires onto the wax. Make the inscription as detailed as you can and as the length of the candle allows. It can be hard to fit long sentences on a small piece of candle, so inscriptions can be brief, just be sure it is clear what you want. For example, if you want to cast a spell for success in my career, inscribe your name and the words "I desire to be successful in my work."

You may find you need a little practice with your knife or pin to make your inscription legible (and take care not to cut yourself), but rest assured the angels have had many eons of practice at trying to decipher these scribbles and they will be able to read just about anything you write!

Anointing the candle with oil is the final stage of preparation. A witch with lots of experience in essential oils might use a special type, such as lavender or citronella, but commonly available vegetable oil is perfect for beginners and will work just as well. Dip your finger into a tiny drop of oil and run it around the base of the candle. Now it is time for the words of your spell, otherwise known as the incantation.

Opening a Spell

A good way to begin a spell is by doing something we call casting a circle. Once you have all the items you need on your altar, take hold of either a quartz crystal or your wand in your right hand and stand quietly in front of your workspace for a moment or two. Wave the crystal or wand over your objects, making the shape of a large circle in the air. This will enclose all of the magick inside the circle and keep out anything negative. There is no need to say anything at this point. It it this is done in silence, it can actually enhance the ritual without adding any confusing elements.

Once your candle is prepared, light it and speak the incantation you inscribed on it, repeating the words seven times. (**Note:** We recommend lighting the candle after you cast the circle so you don't risk setting your clothes on fire.)

Closing a Spell

When you have said your incantation over whichever spell you are casting, always close it down by saying the words "*So mote it be.*" Some witches like to say "*And so it is*" or "*The spell is cast,*" so go with whatever closing phrase you prefer. I like to say a silent thank-you to the angels too when I close a spell down, and I'm sure they smile down on me because of it.

Once you have followed these steps and your magick is under way, leave the candle to burn down and extinguish itself unless the instructions state otherwise. Some spells require you to blow out the flame earlier, but in general, it's best to leave it undisturbed and let it do its thing. (**Note:** Never leave burning candles unattended, and make sure the flames are not close to anything flammable.)

KEY MAGICKAL HERBS

Many herbs have unique magickal properties and, when used in conjunction with a spell, can make the ritual more effective and potent. Here is a list of some of the more popular herbs used by witches. By simply placing these plants on your altar during a ritual, it can help a spell be more successful. Or you might prefer to make your own magickal pouch to change the energies surrounding you. Pouches are traditionally filled with herbs or spices. Pouches or sachets consist of a piece of material, about the size of a handkerchief, that holds the herbs. The pouch is tied at the top with ribbon. You can carry it around with you or hang it above a door or bed, depending on its intended purpose.

ANGELICA (*Angelica*)
Excellent for protection rituals ✦ Connects with your angel or spirit guide ✦ Used in blessings and cleansings ✦ Guards against hexes ✦ Use with a gold candle to summon the Archangel Michael

BAY LEAF (*Laurus nobilis*)
Offers all-around protection ✦ Invokes money ✦ Good for business ✦ Improves psychic abilities ✦ Promotes strength and stamina

BORAGE (*Borago officinalis*)
Brings about peace and harmony ✦ Promotes courage and strength ✦ Increases psychic abilities ✦ Expands businesses or improves one's chances in work-related matters

CHERVIL (*Anthriscus cerefolium*)
Provides protection ✦ Reduces unwanted feelings ✦ Brings a gossip under control ✦ Removes ill-wishing-

CHICORY (*Cichorium intybus*)
For frugality ✦ Removes obstacles ✦ Purifies sacred places ✦ Used in healing spells ✦ Aids in weight loss

CHIVES (*Allium schoenoprasum*)

Offers protection ✦ Drives out negativity ✦ Used in weight-loss spells ✦ Banishes nightmares ✦ Promotes general good health

CLOVER (*Trifolium*)

Breaks hexes and removes negative spirits ✦ Attracts wealth and money ✦ Promotes good luck, happiness, and harmony

COMFREY (*Symphytum*)

Calms emotions ✦ Promotes safe travel ✦ Heals painful emotions ✦ Cultivates beauty ✦ Attracts wealth and money

CORIANDER OR CILANTRO (*Coriandrum sativum*)

For healing spells ✦ Enhances love and relationships ✦ Seeds used for attracting new love ✦ Promotes fertility

DILL (*Anethum graveolens*)

Brings good luck and good fortune ✦ Protects babies ✦ Boosts the sex drive ✦ Promotes success in court cases ✦ Improves well-being ✦ Draws blessings to you ✦ Improves concentration

ECHINACEA (*Echinacea*)

Used in general health spells ✦ Boosts strength and stamina ✦ For healthy babies ✦ To strengthen relationships

FENNEL (*Foeniculum vulgare*)

For healing spells ✦ For cleansing and blessings ✦ Purifies the altar ✦ Brings strength to hopeless situations

FENUGREEK (*Trigonella foenum-graecum*)

Boosts finances ✦ Increases luck and prosperity ✦ Promotes success in business ✦ Used in weight-loss spells

FEVERFEW (*Tanacetum parthenium*)

Improves your mental state ◆ Brings about happiness and joy ◆ Used in rituals for well-being and removing pain

HYSSOP (*Hyssopus officinalis*)

Promotes meditation ◆ Used for cleansing and purification ◆ Boosts creativity ◆ Breaks curses and hexes ◆ Sanctifies altars (infuse the herb with water and sprinkle it over magickal areas)

LEMONGRASS (*Cymbopogon*)

Wards off evil ◆ Removes hexes ◆ Used in love magick to attract romance ◆ Settles disruptive relationships ◆ Calms fractious children ◆ Used in general healing rituals

LEMON VERBENA (*Aloysia citrodora*)

Helps you break bad habits ◆ Boosts willpower ◆ Calms and purifies ◆ Used in beauty treatments

LOVAGE (*Levisticum officinale*)

For love spells ◆ Increases passion in a relationship ◆ Brings happiness and love into families ◆ Used in trinkets and gifts to give to loved ones ◆ Seals friendships

MILK THISTLE (*Silybum marianum*)

Protects you from anything evil ◆ Increases passion ◆ Summons the spirit world ◆ Guards against illness

MINT (*Mentha*)

Used in healing spells ◆ For safe travel ◆ Invites guides and angels ◆ Promotes money and cash flow ◆ Brings about better luck

NETTLE (*Urtica*)

Burn nettle to cleanse altar tools ✦ Protects from dangerous people or places ✦ Casts out evil spirits and ghosts ✦ Hang bundles in your car for protection ✦ Attracts fairies

OREGANO (*Origanum vulgare*)

Brings happiness and protection ✦ Promotes good fortune and prosperity ✦ Used in rituals to get over complicated relationships ✦ Protects the home

PARSLEY (*Petroselinum crispum*)

Used as a charm for luck in competitions ✦ Brings about strength and courage ✦ Twin with turquoise to aid healing ✦ For weddings and other ceremonies ✦ To win a new job ✦ Casts out bad luck and ushers in positivity

SORREL (*Rumex acetosa*)

To enchant ✦ Entices fairies and elves to the garden ✦ Increases luck and good fortune

ST. JOHN'S WORT (*Hypericum perforatum*)

Wards off pain and fever ✦ Banishes or removes hexes ✦ Used in protection spells ✦ Prevents nightmares ✦ Lifts a dark mood

ASTRO—AROMATHERAPY

In recent years, the ancient practice of aromatherapy has reemerged as a legitimate means of enhancing and healing energy. In fact, you've likely seen an essential oil diffuser somewhere in your daily travels—at the doctor's office, in a little boutique, at the spa, in a friend's home. Some aromatherapists swear by using astrological signs as a starting point for finding the most effective essential oils for a person. What do the stars say about your best scents?

ARIES › ROSEMARY Aries is a go-getter and doesn't have time for nonsense. Rosemary has a sharp, direct scent that provides a boost to Aries's already jam-packed day. Mix with some lavender or bergamot to help tame tension.

TAURUS › ROSE Taurus comes charging into any situation with confidence and boldness—just like the strong scent of roses. Both are uniquely strong and cannot be overpowered. Use sandalwood and frankincense as companion oils if feelings of doubt and insecurity start to creep in.

GEMINI › BASIL Strong and versatile, basil mirrors Gemini's intensity and habit of being involved in everything. This scent can be used to boost a weary mind but is equally at home in the kitchen in a variety of recipes. Try using clary sage and rose to bring some focus to your busy days.

CANCER › BLUE CHAMOMILE This sign is all about nurturing others, and blue chamomile matches that energy perfectly. It has a calming nature, like Cancer, and is perfect to soothe the stomach issues that this sign is prone to. Add some cinnamon oil to shake things up and provide a boost of energy.

LEO › JASMINE There is nothing shy about Leo, which is what makes jasmine the perfect scent for this sign. It's indulgent and bold, just like the Leo personality. It's also a definite seasonal scent, reflecting Leo's endless-summer mind-set. Bergamot and ylang-ylang are good companion oils, as they help to ease Leo's occasionally intense irritation.

VIRGO › LAVENDER Virgo personalities are lovely and loving, like lavender itself. They are the first to respond to a crisis of any sort, and the last to consider themselves a hero. This sign is associated with the mother goddesses of the harvest season. Peppermint and cedarwood are nice companion oils to give Virgo a boost of concentration and healing energy to their over-giving selves.

LIBRA › GERANIUM Libra personalities are usually focused on what's fair, what's right, and how to balance the scales. Geranium is used as a balancing scent in aromatherapy, which makes it perfect for this sign. If you find that geranium is too strong for you, add some palmarosa—this is a type of grass that may be more to your liking.

SCORPIO › PATCHOULI Scorpios are known for their deep, sensual energy. Patchouli has been used as an aphrodisiac for centuries, making it the perfect scent for this sign. Ginger and lemon are excellent companions, as they add a zing of freshness and light to patchouli's earthiness.

SAGITTARIUS › BLACK PEPPER Sagittarius doesn't beat around the bush, and neither does black pepper, with its stimulating scent! Sagittarius is full of energy and sometimes says things before thinking. Rosewood can help to smooth out those overexcited edges and bring Sagittarian energy back into balance.

CAPRICORN › VETIVER This sign is like an oldest child: responsible, overachieving, and well rooted. Vetiver is an earthy scent that plays on the ambition and serenity of Capricorns. Amyris mixes well and encourages relaxation when Capricorn has been working too hard!

AQUARIUS › NEROLI Aquarians often appear to be distant, off in their own little worlds—lost in deep thought and happy with their own company. Neroli is a great oil for meditation, to help Aquarius sort out all those thoughts. Marjoram is a good addition and helps to soothe the anxiety that many overthinkers are prone to.

PISCES › LEMON BALM Pisceans are the ultimate water sign, and lemon balm has a high water content, making them a perfect pair. This sign is highly compassionate and absorbs a lot of dark energy from others, and lemon balm helps to ease anxiety and depression. Cinnamon pairs well with lemon balm and encourages Pisces's natural psychic abilities.

NOTES

NOTES

ABOUT THE AUTHORS

Shawn Robbins is the author or coauthor of six books, including *The Holistic Witch*, *Psychic Spellcraft*, *The Witch's Way*, *The Crystal Witch*, *The Good Witch*, and *Wiccapedia*, which is now used as a reference guide in many online Wicca schools, as well as *The Wiccapedia Spell Deck* and *Wiccapedia Journal*—all in the Modern-Day Witch series. She has taught classes about herbs, health, and healing at the New York School of Occult Arts and lectures extensively throughout the country on these subjects. She lives in New York City.

Leanna Greenaway is a popular British clairvoyant who has appeared on TV and radio. She is the author or coauthor of numerous books, including *The Holistic Witch*, *Psychic Spellcraft*, *The Witch's Way*, *The Crystal Witch*, *Wiccapedia*, and *Simply Tarot*, as well as *The Wiccapedia Spell Deck* and *Wiccapedia Journal*. She was a columnist for UK *Fate & Fortune Magazine*. See more at leannagreenaway.info. She lives in South West England.

IMAGE CREDITS

2024

JANUARY 2024

S	M	T	W	T	F	S
	1	2	3	4	5	6
7	8	9	10	11	12	13
14	15	16	17	18	19	20
21	22	23	24	25	26	27
28	29	30	31			

FEBRUARY 2024

S	M	T	W	T	F	S
				1	2	3
4	5	6	7	8	9	10
11	12	13	14	15	16	17
18	19	20	21	22	23	24
25	26	27	28	29		

MARCH 2024

S	M	T	W	T	F	S
					1	2
3	4	5	6	7	8	9
10	11	12	13	14	15	16
17	18	19	20	21	22	23
24	25	26	27	28	29	30
31						

APRIL 2024

S	M	T	W	T	F	S
	1	2	3	4	5	6
7	8	9	10	11	12	13
14	15	16	17	18	19	20
21	22	23	24	25	26	27
28	29	30				

MAY 2024

S	M	T	W	T	F	S
			1	2	3	4
5	6	7	8	9	10	11
12	13	14	15	16	17	18
19	20	21	22	23	24	25
26	27	28	29	30	31	

JUNE 2024

S	M	T	W	T	F	S
						1
2	3	4	5	6	7	8
9	10	11	12	13	14	15
16	17	18	19	20	21	22
23	24	25	26	27	28	29
30						

JULY 2024

S	M	T	W	T	F	S
	1	2	3	4	5	6
7	8	9	10	11	12	13
14	15	16	17	18	19	20
21	22	23	24	25	26	27
28	29	30	31			

AUGUST 2024

S	M	T	W	T	F	S
				1	2	3
4	5	6	7	8	9	10
11	12	13	14	15	16	17
18	19	20	21	22	23	24
25	26	27	28	29	30	31

SEPTEMBER 2024

S	M	T	W	T	F	S
1	2	3	4	5	6	7
8	9	10	11	12	13	14
15	16	17	18	19	20	21
22	23	24	25	26	27	28
29	30					

OCTOBER 2024

S	M	T	W	T	F	S
		1	2	3	4	5
6	7	8	9	10	11	12
13	14	15	16	17	18	19
20	21	22	23	24	25	26
27	28	29	30	31		

NOVEMBER 2024

S	M	T	W	T	F	S
					1	2
3	4	5	6	7	8	9
10	11	12	13	14	15	16
17	18	19	20	21	22	23
24	25	26	27	28	29	30

DECEMBER 2024

S	M	T	W	T	F	S
1	2	3	4	5	6	7
8	9	10	11	12	13	14
15	16	17	18	19	20	21
22	23	24	25	26	27	28
29	30	31				

2025

JANUARY 2025

S	M	T	W	T	F	S
			1	2	3	4
5	6	7	8	9	10	11
12	13	14	15	16	17	18
19	20	21	22	23	24	25
26	27	28	29	30	31	

FEBRUARY 2025

S	M	T	W	T	F	S
						1
2	3	4	5	6	7	8
9	10	11	12	13	14	15
16	17	18	19	20	21	22
23	24	25	26	27	28	29
30						

MARCH 2025

S	M	T	W	T	F	S
						1
2	3	4	5	6	7	8
9	10	11	12	13	14	15
16	17	18	19	20	21	22
23	24	25	26	27	28	29
30	31					

APRIL 2025

S	M	T	W	T	F	S
		1	2	3		
4	5	6	7	8	9	10
11	12	13	14	15	16	17
18	19	20	21	22	23	24
25	26	27	28	29	30	

MAY 2025

S	M	T	W	T	F	S
				1	2	3
4	5	6	7	8	9	10
11	12	13	14	15	16	17
18	19	20	21	22	23	24
25	26	27	28	29	30	31

JUNE 2025

S	M	T	W	T	F	S
1	2	3	4	5	6	7
8	9	10	11	12	13	14
15	16	17	18	19	20	21
22	23	24	25	26	27	28
29	30					

JULY 2025

S	M	T	W	T	F	S
		1	2	3		
4	5	6	7	8	9	10
11	12	13	14	15	16	17
18	19	20	21	22	23	24
25	26	27	28	29	30	31

AUGUST 2025

S	M	T	W	T	F	S
1	2	3	4	5	6	7
8	9	10	11	12	13	14
15	16	17	18	19	20	21
22	23	24	25	26	27	28
29	30	31				

SEPTEMBER 2025

S	M	T	W	T	F	S
	1	2	3	4		
5	6	7	8	9	10	11
12	13	14	15	16	17	18
19	20	21	22	23	24	25
26	27	28	29	30		

OCTOBER 2025

S	M	T	W	T	F	S
			1	2		
3	4	5	6	7	8	9
10	11	12	13	14	15	16
17	18	19	20	21	22	23
24	25	26	27	28	29	30
31						

NOVEMBER 2025

S	M	T	W	T	F	S
	1	2	3	4	5	6
7	8	9	10	11	12	13
14	15	16	17	18	19	20
21	22	23	24	25	26	27
28	29	30				

DECEMBER 2025

S	M	T	W	T	F	S
	1	2	3	4		
5	6	7	8	9	10	11
12	13	14	15	16	17	18
19	20	21	22	23	24	25
26	27	28	29	30	31